Everyday
Dinner Ideas

Also by Addie Gundry

No-Bake Desserts:
103 Easy Recipes for No-Bake Cookies, Bars, and Treats

Family Favorite Casseroles:
103 Comforting Breakfast Casseroles, Dinner Ideas,
and Desserts Everyone Will Love

Easy Cookie Recipes:
103 Best Recipes for Chocolate Chip Cookies, Cake Mix Creations,
Bars, and Holiday Treats Everyone Will Love

Everyday Dinner Ideas

103 *Easy Recipes for Chicken, Pasta, and*
Other Dishes Everyone Will Love

Addie Gundry

St. Martin's Griffin ﾝ New York

To Deb, a super mom.

Thank you for becoming my family and

for bringing joy into our lives every day. Thank you for

showing me what dinner could really mean.

EVERYDAY DINNER IDEAS. Text and photographs copyright © 2017 Prime Publishing LLC. All rights reserved. Printed in the United States of America. For information, address St. Martin's Press, 175 Fifth Avenue, New York, N.Y. 10010.

www.stmartins.com

Photographs by Megan Von Schönhoff

The Library of Congress Cataloging-in-Publication Data is available upon request.

ISBN 978-1-250-13231-4 (trade paperback)
ISBN 978-1-250-13232-1 (e-book)

Our books may be purchased in bulk for promotional, educational, or business use. Please contact your local bookseller or the Macmillan Corporate and Premium Sales Department at 1-800-221-7945, extension 5442, or by e-mail at MacmillanSpecialMarkets@macmillan.com.

First Edition: November 2017

10 9 8 7 6 5 4 3 2 1

Contents

5 Pasta and Vegetarian

6 Side Dishes

7 Grilling Made Easy

8 Dessert

Introduction

Dinner. That word has many meanings. It can be that small window of time you have to feed the kids (and maybe yourself, if you're lucky) and race against the clock, hoping to convince your children to eat their broccoli before bath time. On the flip side, dinner can mean a first date, an anniversary, or even a birthday. Dinner can be a magnificent occasion, where the table is set with your finest china and crisply ironed linens. You can eat at 6 p.m. or 10 p.m. You can order pizza or poach lobster. Dinner is what you make of it.

When I was a small child, my farm family in Minnesota put a lot of meaning into what we called supper. But as I got older, life changed (divorce, graduation, moving . . . well, you know how it goes). I do remember sit-down dinner at boarding school, which felt more like a chore with assigned seating and forced conversation, and at the other extreme, dinner in college, which consisted of frozen yogurt and a library book. When I began working in restaurants, dinner became the leftover French fries after I plated a dish. Late-night dinners included Swedish fish and pretzels. As a formally trained chef, it's odd to think that it took so many years for me to begin making proper dinners—and to begin enjoying it.

I will never forget making my now-husband our first date-night dinner, helping my mother-in-law during our first Christmas together, and making my first turkey on Thanksgiving. When my husband was in business school, dinners for six became dinners for a dozen as new friends came to the door, and when it was Slow Cooker Pulled Pork (page 95) night, our home was busting at the seams. Now, dinner prep on Sunday is one of my favorite activities, planning a menu for a party beats that, and sitting down with a glass of wine, friends, and family is, hands down, what I love most about our life.

My favorite dinner is one where all the food goes on the table at once. It begins as a beautiful spread, and in the end, it's a dazzling mess of wine stains, crumbs, empty plates, and full bellies. Not all dinners need to be complicated or time-consuming, but it's a time that gives you an opportunity to take a breath. You can't skip it, yet I have learned that it can be stressful, and I am here to tell you that it doesn't have to be. I have created 103 recipes that are foolproof and that will excite kids, but that will also give reason for you to sit back and have a glass of wine on date night. Why 103? When you come to my house for dinner, I want you to know you can always bring a friend or two or three . . . and for those who have been to my home, you know firsthand that guests tend to multiply as the food continues to come out of the oven and cocktails continue to be poured. One hundred recipes felt too rigid, too finite. By adding in the extra three, it became more welcoming, a reminder that there is always more room at the table. I have learned that dinner has a whole other meaning to it: a good one. The day is over, the night has begun, and wherever you are sitting and whoever you're with, thank your lucky stars.

—Addie Gundry

1

Appetizers and Salads

How do you start your meal? If I could, I would eat appetizers
all day. This chapter is a collection of my favorites.
From antipasti to fried pickles to barbecue meatballs,
there is something for every occasion.

Bacon-Wrapped Smokies

Yield: Serves 6 | Prep Time: 20 minutes | Cook Time: 30 to 35 minutes

With smoky bacon and caramelized sugar, these beef cocktail sausages are wrapped up for flavor with a kick. They're crispy and spicy with a little cayenne to give you the texture and taste that will keep you going back for more. Served with honey mustard and a dash of red pepper flakes, each is a perfect bite.

INGREDIENTS

¼ cup packed light brown sugar

Pinch cayenne pepper

1 (16-ounce) package beef cocktail sausages, drained and rinsed

8 slices bacon, cut into quarters

1 tablespoon maple syrup

½ cup honey mustard

¼ teaspoon red pepper flakes

DIRECTIONS

1. Preheat the oven to 350°F. Line a baking sheet with parchment paper. Combine the brown sugar and cayenne pepper on a small plate.

2. Wrap each cocktail sausage in a quarter slice of bacon and dredge in the brown sugar mixture, pressing to coat well. Place the sausages seam side down on the baking sheet. Drizzle the maple syrup over the sausages.

3. Bake until the brown sugar has caramelized and the bacon is crisp, 30 to 35 minutes. Meanwhile, in a small bowl, mix the honey mustard and red pepper flakes.

4. Serve the sausages with the honey mustard mixture for dipping.

NOTES

If you don't have prepared honey mustard on hand or can't find it at the store, just whisk ¼ cup honey, ¼ cup mayonnaise, ¼ cup Dijon mustard, and 1 tablespoon white distilled vinegar together.

Barbecue Meatballs

Yield: Makes 36 meatballs | Prep Time: 25 minutes | Cook Time: 35 to 40 minutes

Meatballs are one of my favorite dishes, and I like them even better when they are bite-size. It makes them oh-so-poppable and perfect to set out on the kitchen counter while preparing the main course.

INGREDIENTS

1 cup quick-cooking oats

¾ cup finely chopped white onion

½ cup plus 2 tablespoons half-and-half

1 large egg, beaten

2 garlic cloves, minced

1 teaspoon kosher salt

1 teaspoon chili powder

¼ teaspoon freshly ground black pepper

1½ pounds ground beef or turkey

1 cup ketchup

¾ cup packed light brown sugar

½ teaspoon liquid smoke (optional)

¼ teaspoon espresso powder

DIRECTIONS

1. Preheat the oven to 350°F and grease a wire rack set in a rimmed baking sheet.

2. Combine the oats, ½ cup of the onion, the half-and-half, egg, garlic, salt, chili powder, and pepper in a large bowl. Crumble the beef or turkey over the mixture and mix well. Roll the mixture into 1-inch balls and place on the rack. Bake for 20 minutes, or until the meat is no longer pink inside.

3. While the meatballs are cooking, combine the ketchup, brown sugar, remaining ¼ cup onion, liquid smoke, if using, and espresso powder in a saucepan. Bring to a boil and simmer for 2 to 3 minutes.

4. Remove the meatballs from the oven and drizzle the sauce over the meatballs. Cook the meatballs for an additional 15 to 20 minutes, until the internal temperature reaches 160°F for ground beef or 165°F for ground turkey. Arrange the meatballs on a platter or in a bowl and serve.

Olive and Mozzarella Antipasti

Yield: Serves 4 | Prep Time: 5 minutes | Marinate Time: 2 hours

I could eat this appetizer every day! Delicious olives and roasted red peppers drenched in olive oil, basil, and lemon—doesn't that just sound heavenly? The lemon adds a hint of tang that perfectly complements the rich mozzarella cheese. It's the perfect dish to share, to munch on, and to carry you through 'til dinner is ready.

INGREDIENTS

1 cup pitted olives, any variety

1 cup bocconcini (bite-size mozzarella balls)

1 cup sliced fresh basil (thin ribbons)

1 (16-ounce) jar red peppers, drained and chopped into bite-size pieces

1 cup olive oil

1 lemon, halved and sliced thin

1 shallot, minced

1 teaspoon red pepper flakes

½ teaspoon salt

½ teaspoon freshly ground black pepper

DIRECTIONS

Combine all the ingredients in a large bowl. Let marinate for at least 2 hours at room temperature before serving.

Mango-Tomato Salsa

Yield: Makes 2 cups; serves 4 to 6 | Prep Time: 15 minutes | Chill Time: 1 hour

I volunteer as a chef-instructor for a program in Chicago that teaches first-graders about healthy eating. We learn about ingredients and make recipes—it's a blast! Many of the kids have never seen a mango before I come to visit, and some are hesitant to try it. After helping to make this deliciously simple salsa, they inevitably say that can't wait to make it at home with Mom and Dad. Serve this salsa with tortilla chips.

INGREDIENTS

2 mangoes, peeled and cut into ½-inch pieces

2 plum tomatoes, cut into ½-inch pieces

½ red onion, finely minced

¼ cup minced fresh cilantro

⅓ cup lime juice

Salt and freshly ground black pepper

DIRECTIONS

Combine all of the ingredients in a large bowl and stir to coat evenly with lime juice. Season with salt and pepper to taste. Refrigerate for at least 1 hour before serving.

Parmesan Ranch Oyster Crackers

Yield: Makes 5½ cups oyster crackers | Prep Time: 5 minutes | Cook Time: 5 minutes

This was my grandfather's beloved recipe. There was never a time that I recall when we didn't have these zesty oyster crackers at the farm or cabin. As a young aspiring chef, I thought it was so innovative that he transformed these plain little crackers into something amazing.

INGREDIENTS

1 (9-ounce) bag oyster crackers

⅓ cup olive oil

1 (1-ounce) packet ranch dressing and seasoning mix

¼ cup grated Parmesan cheese

DIRECTIONS

1. Preheat the oven to 200°F. In a large bowl, combine the oyster crackers with the oil and ranch seasoning. Stir until well coated.

2. Pour onto a rimmed baking sheet and bake for 5 minutes, until slightly golden brown and the seasoning adheres. Remove from the oven and allow to cool for at least 5 minutes.

3. Top with the cheese, transfer to a bowl, and serve.

NOTES

These are great warm or at room temperature. Stored in an airtight container, they will keep for four or five days—if they last that long!

Party Mix

Yield: Serves 8 to 10 | Prep Time: 10 minutes | Cook Time: 10 minutes

When I taught at The Food Business School at The Culinary Institute of America, we created a three-day workshop in which, using design-thinking methods, we redesigned snack mix. We experimented with sweet flavor profiles, spicy ones, and even combinations of the two. In the end, it's safe to say that I have made about a gazillion party mixes, and this is the one that ranks the best with everyone we have asked!

INGREDIENTS

3 cups Wheat Chex cereal

2 cups mini pretzel twists

2 cups popped popcorn

½ cup Worcestershire sauce

4 tablespoons unsalted butter, melted

1 tablespoon Jane's Krazy Mixed-Up Salt (or Lawry's Seasoned Salt)

1 teaspoon sugar

1 teaspoon garlic powder

DIRECTIONS

1. Preheat the oven to 250°F. In a large bowl, combine the cereal, pretzels, and popcorn.

2. In a separate bowl, whisk together the Worcestershire sauce, melted butter, Mixed-Up Salt, sugar, and garlic powder. Pour over the cereal mixture and stir to combine.

3. Spread the mixture out on a baking sheet and bake for 10 minutes. Transfer to a large bowl and serve.

Cilantro Pepper Queso Dip

Yield: Serves 4 | Prep Time: 10 minutes | Cook Time: 10 minutes

Often during my boarding school days, the most exciting outing my friends and I made was to Chili's. Four to six of us girls would get on the white school bus shuttle and head over to the mall to eat queso dip. It was always full of flavor (and grease) and served with a ton of chips. To this day, I'm nostalgic for that cheesy yellow dip, so here's my best rendition of that fond dinner memory.

INGREDIENTS

½ cup half-and-half

1½ cups shredded Oaxaca or mozzarella cheese (see Notes)

1 cup shredded cheddar cheese

1 tablespoon chopped canned jalapeños (see note)

1 teaspoon hot sauce

½ teaspoon dried oregano

¼ teaspoon ground cumin

Pinch salt

For serving:

Chopped tomatoes

Fresh cilantro

Sliced jalapeño, banana, or bell peppers, seeds and membranes removed

Tortilla chips

DIRECTIONS

1. Preheat the oven to broil. In an 8-inch ovenproof skillet, bring the half-and-half to a very low boil over medium-high heat. Reduce the heat to low and whisk in the Oaxaca and cheddar cheeses until smooth. Add the canned jalapeños, hot sauce, oregano, cumin, and salt and continue to whisk until smooth.

2. Place the pan under the broiler for 3 to 5 minutes, until the top just begins to brown and bubble. Garnish with tomatoes, cilantro, and sliced peppers and serve immediately with chips for dipping.

NOTES

The recipe can be spiced up to your taste by adding more jalapeños or hot sauce or adding a pinch of red pepper flakes to the cheese mixture.

Oaxaca cheese and canned jalapeños are available in most supermarkets or in Mexican markets; if you can't find Oaxaca cheese, mozzarella makes a good substitute. Or you can substitute an equal amount of pepper Jack cheese and omit the canned jalapeños.

Seven-Layer Mexican Dip

Yield: Serves 4 | Prep Time: 15 minutes | Chill Time: 1 hour

One of the easiest appetizers you can make is a layered dip. Layer a few tasty ingredients, chill them, and then serve with chips. There are probably a million different versions of a seven-layer dip, but this one has a bit of a kick that keeps everyone coming back for more. Have plenty of tortilla chips on hand!

INGREDIENTS

½ cup salsa

1 (16-ounce) can refried beans

1 cup sour cream

1 (15.25-ounce) can whole kernel corn, drained

3 banana peppers, sliced

1 (2.5-ounce) can black olives, drained well and sliced

1 avocado, sliced

½ teaspoon salt

½ teaspoon freshly ground black pepper

Chopped fresh cilantro

DIRECTIONS

Pour ¼ cup of the salsa into a 2-quart bowl and spread the refried beans on top. Gently spread the sour cream over the refried beans, then add the remaining ¼ cup of the salsa. Sprinkle the top evenly with the corn, then the peppers, black olives, and avocado slices. Sprinkle with the salt, pepper, and cilantro, chill for at least an hour, and serve.

Spinach Parmesan Dip

Yield: Serves 6 to 8 | Prep Time: 10 minutes | Cook Time: 20 minutes

I love this as a hot appetizer as well as a dinner topping! Make it for a crowd and save what's left for dinner the next day. Just top a grilled chicken breast with the dip, and it will melt on top like butter to make a fun, new weeknight flavor. Serve with slices of baguette, chips, or crackers.

INGREDIENTS

1 (14-ounce) can artichoke hearts in water, drained

10 ounces frozen chopped spinach, thawed and well drained

1 cup finely grated Parmesan cheese

¾ cup mayonnaise

½ cup shredded mozzarella cheese

1 (0.7-ounce) packet dry Italian salad dressing mix

1 garlic clove, finely minced

DIRECTIONS

1. Preheat the oven to 350°F. Spray a 9-inch deep-dish pie plate with cooking spray. Coarsely chop the artichokes and place them in a medium bowl.

2. Place the spinach in a colander and press with a spoon to remove excess moisture, then transfer to a clean non–terry cloth kitchen towel and roll and squeeze to remove as much moisture as possible.

3. Add the dried spinach into the bowl with the artichokes, then add all but 2 tablespoons of the Parmesan, the mayonnaise, mozzarella, Italian dressing mix, and garlic. Stir to combine, then spread in the prepared pie plate.

4. Top with the reserved Parmesan and bake for 20 minutes until lightly browned and heated through. Serve.

NOTES

To make ahead, assemble the dip, cover with plastic wrap, and refrigerate until needed. Bake straight from the refrigerator, adding 5 minutes to the bake time.

Grilled Romaine with Blue Cheese Dressing

Yield: Serves 4 | Prep Time: 5 minutes | Cook Time: 5 minutes

I learned about grilled romaine from my mother-in-law, and it's to die for. The slightly wilted and almost-warm lettuce with a grill char stands up to the thick and creamy blue cheese dressing and heirloom tomatoes. It's perfect for a crowd or just for you.

INGREDIENTS

2 romaine hearts

¼ cup olive oil

1 cup blue cheese dressing

1 cup crumbled blue cheese

2 tomatoes, sliced thin

Salt and freshly ground black pepper

DIRECTIONS

1. Preheat the grill to medium-high heat (about 450°F).

2. Slice the romaine hearts in half lengthwise and brush with the olive oil. Place the romaine hearts, cut side down, on the grill and cook for 5 minutes, until charred and wilted.

3. Transfer to a platter and top with the dressing, crumbled blue cheese, and tomato slices. Sprinkle with salt and pepper to taste and serve.

NOTES

If you don't have access to a grill, you can use a grill pan on the stove, preheated over high heat for 5 minutes.

Zesty Lemon Salmon on Greens

Yield: Serves 4 | Prep Time: 5 minutes | Cook Time: 10 to 15 minutes

Salmon is delicious served cold on a salad at night, and all you have to do is top mixed greens with a balsamic vinaigrette. If you are not in the mood for greens, place the fish on a toasted bun with a little aioli and lettuce for a delicious weekday sandwich.

INGREDIENTS

Salmon

4 (4-ounce) skin-on salmon fillets

1 teaspoon red pepper flakes

½ teaspoon salt

½ teaspoon freshly ground black pepper

1 lemon, halved and sliced

Vinaigrette

¼ cup olive oil

¼ cup balsamic vinegar

1 tablespoon Dijon mustard

1 shallot, minced

4 cups mixed greens

Fresh dill, for garnish

DIRECTIONS

1. For the salmon: Preheat the oven to broil. Line a baking sheet with aluminum foil.

2. Place the salmon skin-side down on the baking sheet and sprinkle with the red pepper flakes, salt, and pepper. Arrange the lemon slices over the fish. Broil for 10 minutes, until the salmon is cooked through.

3. For the vinaigrette: Meanwhile, combine the oil, vinegar, mustard, and shallot in a jar with a lid and shake. Divide the mixed greens among 4 plates and drizzle some of the vinaigrette over the greens. Place a salmon fillet on each plate and serve, garnished with fresh dill.

NOTES

I like to make salmon on Sunday to eat later in the week. Put in a sealed container and store in the fridge for up to 3 days.

Shrimp Cocktail

Yield: Serves 4 | Prep Time: 5 minutes | Cook Time: 3 minutes

Peel-and-eat shrimp are simply the greatest. I have fond summer memories of eating fresh shrimp by the beach, and every Christmas Eve my family loves to make this special holiday appetizer. No matter what time of year you eat them, shrimp are so versatile and just the most delicious way to start the evening.

INGREDIENTS

¼ cup lemon juice, plus lemon wedges for serving

1 cup ketchup

2 tablespoons horseradish

1 shallot, minced

1 garlic clove, minced

¼ teaspoon Worcestershire sauce

¼ teaspoon hot sauce

Salt and freshly ground black pepper

1 pound large shrimp, unpeeled

DIRECTIONS

1. Bring 1 gallon water and the lemon juice to a boil in a large stockpot.

2. Meanwhile, stir the ketchup, horseradish, shallot, garlic, Worcestershire sauce, and hot sauce in a medium bowl to combine. Season with salt and pepper to taste; refrigerate until needed.

3. Add the shrimp to the boiling water and cook until they curl and turn a light pink, about 3 minutes. Drain and let cool to room temperature.

4. Peel the shrimp and place in a bath of ice water to cool, about 5 minutes. Serve with the chilled cocktail sauce and lemon wedges.

Chicken-Slaw Salad

Yield: Serves 4 | Prep Time: 10 minutes | Cook Time: n/a

Rotisserie chicken is my secret ingredient and a good friend to the frazzled home chef. Whenever I am in a hurry, I pick one up at the store and add it to anything and everything—including pasta, cold salads, and hot soups—to make a great meal. I love this healthy salad because it's a refreshing summer dish, and the leftovers are just as good the next day.

INGREDIENTS

¼ cup olive oil

¼ cup champagne vinegar

1 tablespoon Dijon mustard

1 shallot, minced

Meat from 1 rotisserie chicken, shredded

1 (14-ounce) package coleslaw mix

1 cup raisins

½ teaspoon salt

½ teaspoon freshly ground black pepper

DIRECTIONS

1. Combine the oil, vinegar, mustard, and minced shallot in a jar with a lid and shake well.

2. Combine the shredded chicken, coleslaw mix, raisins, salt, and pepper in a large bowl. Add the vinaigrette and stir to combine. Divide into 4 bowls and serve immediately.

Fried Pickles

Yield: Serves 4 | Prep Time: 10 minutes | Cook Time: 20 to 25 minutes

What I love about this recipe is that it is so easy to make, it keeps everyone engaged, and there is not a lot of fuss. In fact, the other night I was explaining the two-step process to my friends and my handy trick to remember exactly how easy the process is: Everyone in the (buttermilk) pool, but everyone dries off separately (in the cornmeal). That means you can dump the pickles together in the buttermilk and let them soak. You just have to remember to pull them out one by one to dip in the cornmeal before frying.

INGREDIENTS

1 (24-ounce) jar dill pickles (spears or rounds)

1 cup buttermilk

1 cup cornmeal

½ teaspoon salt

½ teaspoon freshly ground black pepper

½ teaspoon cayenne pepper

Olive oil

DIRECTIONS

1. Drain the pickles in a colander and set aside.

2. Place the buttermilk in a bowl. Place the cornmeal, salt, pepper, and cayenne pepper in a separate bowl and mix well.

3. Drop the pickles in the buttermilk to coat. One at a time, transfer the pickles to the cornmeal and coat. Place on a plate and set aside.

4. Pour enough oil into a large, deep frying pan to reach a depth of 1 inch and heat over medium-high heat.

5. Place 6 pickle pieces at a time in the oil and fry them for 5 to 6 minutes until golden. Be sure to flip the pickles about halfway though cooking to brown both sides. Drain the pickles on paper towels and serve immediately.

NOTE

These are tasty served with a spicy ranch dressing: just combine 1 cup ranch dressing with 1 to 2 teaspoons of your favorite hot sauce.

Fish Tacos

Yield: Serves 4 | Prep Time: 25 minutes | Cook Time: 10 minutes

I made these with a group of girlfriends at a DIY taco party. Everyone brought their favorite taco fixings, and we had a blast showing each other our recipes and, of course, eating them up. You can prep everything ahead of time and allow guests to assemble the tacos while socializing, making entertaining easy.

INGREDIENTS

4 cups shredded green cabbage

5 tablespoons minced fresh cilantro

3 scallions, sliced thin

2 tablespoons cider vinegar

2 teaspoons canola oil

Salt and freshly ground black pepper

¼ cup light mayonnaise

1½ teaspoons lime juice, plus lime wedges for serving

1 teaspoon minced canned chipotle chile in adobo sauce

⅛ teaspoon garlic salt

2 teaspoons chili powder

½ teaspoon ground coriander

¼ teaspoon ground cumin

2 pounds tilapia fillets

8 (6-inch) flour tortillas, warmed

DIRECTIONS

1. Preheat the oven to 400°F. Line a baking sheet with parchment paper.

2. Toss the cabbage, ¼ cup of the cilantro, the scallions, vinegar, 1 teaspoon of the oil, and ¼ teaspoon salt together in a bowl. In a separate bowl, combine the remaining tablespoon of cilantro, the mayonnaise, lime juice, chipotle chile, and garlic salt and season with salt and pepper to taste. Set both aside for serving.

3. Combine the chili powder, coriander, cumin, ⅛ teaspoon salt, and ⅛ teaspoon pepper in a bowl. Pat the tilapia dry with paper towels, brush with the remaining teaspoon of oil, and rub evenly with the spice mixture.

4. Place the tilapia on the baking sheet. Bake for 10 minutes. Cut apart into bite-size pieces with a fork and knife.

5. Smear each tortilla with ½ tablespoon of the mayonnaise mixture and top with some of the cabbage slaw and a few pieces of fish. Serve with lime wedges.

2

Soups and Stews

Soups and stews are an underrated dinner option. Make
them ahead of time and enjoy them all week long with a warm
baguette, a few crackers, or a salad. They're everything
you need in a bowl of belly-warming goodness.

Chicken and Wild Rice Soup

Yield: Serves 6 to 8 | Prep Time: 10 minutes | Cook Time: 30 minutes

My family owns a cabin in northern Minnesota where wild rice grows. I love spending time there, right on Lake Superior, with freshly caught walleye and big, juicy blueberries in the summer. The wild rice is as good as it gets, and this soup is one of my favorite examples of bountiful recipes coming straight out of nature. Serve this soup with a loaf of crusty bread.

INGREDIENTS

2 tablespoons unsalted butter

2 carrots, peeled and sliced ¼ inch thick

4 celery stalks, sliced ¼ inch thick

1 onion, diced into ¼-inch pieces

4 cups low-sodium chicken broth

2 cups sliced cremini mushrooms

1 bay leaf

½ cup wild rice, rinsed and drained

Salt and freshly ground black pepper

2 cups cooked and shredded chicken

1 cup half-and-half

DIRECTIONS

1. In a large heavy-bottomed saucepan, combine the butter, carrots, celery, and onion and cook over medium-high heat. Cook until the vegetables begin to soften and the onion is translucent. Add the chicken broth, mushrooms, and bay leaf and bring to a boil.

2. Add the wild rice, reduce the heat to low, and simmer for 30 minutes or until the rice is tender but still chewy. Season with salt and pepper to taste. Add in the chicken and half-and-half; stir for 3 minutes to heat through. Remove from the stovetop and remove the bay leaf. Let cool for 3 minutes and serve.

Taco Soup

Yield: Serves 4 to 6 | Prep Time: 10 minutes | Cook Time: 20 to 25 minutes

I love making this taco soup because of its easy variations. The base of the soup opens itself up for many flavorful additions. In fact, every time I make this soup, I add a little something different, from various veggies to different bean options. And serving it provides just as many options. My husband pours it on top of rice, making a burrito-type bowl, while I just eat it as is and dip a few chips in!

INGREDIENTS

1 tablespoon olive oil

1 pound lean ground beef

1 (1-ounce) packet low-sodium taco seasoning

½ (1-ounce) packet ranch dressing and seasoning mix

1 tablespoon dried oregano

1 red bell pepper, chopped

½ white onion, chopped

2 cups low-sodium chicken broth

1 (15-ounce) can black beans, drained and rinsed

1 (10-ounce) can tomatoes with green chiles

1 (4.5-ounce) can diced green chiles

1 cup frozen corn

1 teaspoon salt

1 teaspoon freshly ground black pepper

2 cups shredded cheddar cheese

Tortilla chips

DIRECTIONS

1. In a large soup pot, heat the oil over medium-high heat. Add the ground beef and cook until it begins to brown. Add the taco seasoning, ranch seasoning, and oregano and cook, stirring, until the meat is cooked through.

2. Add the bell pepper and onion and sauté for 5 minutes until the vegetables are soft. Add the broth, beans, tomatoes with green chiles, diced green chiles, corn, salt, and pepper. Bring to a boil, then reduce the heat to low and simmer for 10 to 15 minutes.

3. Turn the heat off and add the cheese ½ cup at a time, stirring with each addition. Serve with tortilla chips.

Beef Stew

Yield: Serves 8 | Prep Time: 15 minutes | Cook Time: 1½ hours

After growing up on a farm in Minnesota, I have always relished the smell of a simmering beef stew. Beef stew, rich and hearty in the winter (or summer), fills the home with a savory smell that reminds me of cozy nights with family. To give this stew a "simmered all day" flavor, I use V8 juice. It adds a great nutritional boost without any extra work.

INGREDIENTS

2 tablespoons olive oil

1½ pounds beef chuck, trimmed and cut into 2-inch pieces

1 pound baby carrots, halved crosswise

1 cup chopped onion

1 cup dry red wine

1 (28-ounce) can whole tomatoes

2 cups V8 juice

Salt and freshly ground black pepper

1 pound Yukon Gold potatoes, cut into ½-inch pieces

DIRECTIONS

1. In a large soup pot, heat the oil over medium-high heat. Brown the meat on all sides in batches. Drain, remove from the pot, and set aside.

2. Add the carrots and onions to the empty pot and cook until the onions are translucent. Deglaze the pot with red wine by pouring it into the hot pot and scraping the brown bits from the sides. Return the beef to the pot, including any juices that accumulated. Bring to a simmer and add the tomatoes, V8 juice, and salt and pepper to taste. Simmer for 1 hour.

3. Add the potatoes and simmer until all of the veggies and the meat are tender, about 10 minutes. Serve.

Slow Cooker Chicken Noodle Soup

Yield: Serves 8 | Prep Time: 20 minutes | Cook Time: 6 hours, non-active

It could be argued that the most comforting meal around is chicken noodle soup. It's not just the warmth and the steam that billows out of the bowl, but the texture of each ingredient as you slurp and swallow the warm chicken broth. What makes this recipe so good is the fall-apart-tender chicken, and it's the slow-cooking method that accomplishes this. No need to stand over a stove to make your favorite winter remedy.

INGREDIENTS

1½ pounds boneless, skinless chicken breasts

6 cups low-sodium chicken broth

1 cup water

5 carrots, peeled and sliced ¼ inch thick

1 yellow onion, cut into ½-inch pieces

5 celery stalks, cut into ¼-inch pieces

1 cup frozen peas

3 tablespoons extra-virgin olive oil

5 garlic cloves, minced

1 tablespoon lemon juice

½ teaspoon minced fresh rosemary or 2 teaspoons dried

2 bay leaves

Salt and freshly ground black pepper

1 cup egg noodles

DIRECTIONS

1. Combine the chicken breasts, chicken broth, water, carrots, onion, celery, peas, olive oil, garlic, lemon juice, rosemary, and bay leaves in a 6-quart slow cooker and season with salt and pepper. Cook for 6 hours on low. Discard the bay leaves. Heat a large pot of water to a boil. Add the egg noodles and salt and cook according to package directions. Drain and reserve.

2. Remove the chicken breasts and shred with 2 forks. Return to the slow cooker, add the egg noodles, and heat through for 5 minutes. Serve.

Easy Cheesy Loaded Potato Soup

Yield: Serves 4 to 6 | Prep Time: 10 minutes | Cook Time: 20 minutes

Potatoes are my favorite vegetable. Not because I love French fries (although I do!) but because their hearty, familiar taste warms me up from head to toe, especially when baked or mashed and then combined with butter or olive oil, salt, and pepper. This soup has that buttery baked potato taste and is as creamy as can be.

INGREDIENTS

2 tablespoons all-purpose flour

2 cups chicken broth

4 strips bacon, roughly chopped

2 celery stalks, chopped

1 large shallot, chopped

2 garlic cloves, minced

Salt and freshly ground black pepper

2 cups half-and-half

1 (20-ounce) bag frozen Southern-style hash browns

2 cups shredded sharp cheddar cheese

2 tablespoons chopped scallions

Fresh basil, for garnish (optional)

DIRECTIONS

1. In a small bowl, whisk the flour with ¼ cup broth. Set aside.

2. Cook the bacon in a large soup pot over medium heat until crisp. Remove the bacon to a paper towel–lined plate and set aside. Drain all but 2 tablespoons of bacon fat from the pot.

3. Add the celery, shallot, and garlic to the pot and sauté until soft. Season with salt and pepper.

4. Add the remaining 1¾ cups broth, half-and-half, and hash browns. Bring to a boil, stirring occasionally. Slowly drizzle in the flour/broth mixture while stirring. Reduce the heat to low and simmer until thickened and the potatoes are tender, 10 to 15 minutes.

5. Remove from the heat and stir in the cheese a handful at a time, making sure one handful is combined before adding another. Stir in the bacon and the scallions. Serve, garnished with fresh basil if desired.

Old-Fashioned Chicken and Dumplings

Yield: Serves 6 to 8 | Prep Time: 15 minutes | Cook Time: 1 hour

Dumplings can seem intimidating, but they don't have to be. These are so easy to make, and this dish is perfect when you're looking to snuggle up under a blanket and chow down on something warm during a brisk winter evening.

INGREDIENTS

Soup

1 tablespoon olive oil

2 boneless, skinless chicken breasts, cut into 1-inch pieces

½ large onion, cut into ½-inch pieces

2 celery stalks, sliced ½-inch thick

2 carrots, peeled and sliced ½-inch thick

4 cups low-sodium chicken broth

2 garlic cloves, minced

1 bay leaf

Salt and freshly ground black pepper

1 cup frozen peas

Dumplings

1½ cups all-purpose flour

2 teaspoons baking powder

½ teaspoon salt

¼ teaspoon freshly ground black pepper

3 tablespoons vegetable shortening

¾ cup cold whole milk

DIRECTIONS

1. For the soup: Heat the oil in a large soup pot over medium heat. Add the chicken and cook until all sides are lightly golden brown. Add the onion, celery, and carrots and cook until the vegetables are tender and the onion is translucent, about 5 minutes. Add the broth, garlic, and bay leaf and season with salt and pepper; bring to a boil.

2. Reduce the heat to a simmer and cook uncovered for 20 minutes, or until the chicken is cooked through. Stir in the frozen peas and return to a gentle simmer.

3. For the dumplings: While the soup is simmering, whisk the flour, baking powder, salt, and pepper together in a medium bowl. Add the shortening and, using a pastry cutter or 2 forks, mix until the shortening is the size of small peas. Stir in the milk. For lighter, fluffier dumplings, be sure not to overmix.

4. Drop the dough by large spoonfuls (about 2 tablespoons each) onto the simmering soup. Cook uncovered for 10 minutes. Cover and cook for an additional 10 minutes. The dumplings will puff up and float as they cook. Remove from the heat, remove the bay leaf, and let cool for 5 minutes. Serve, topping each bowl with 2 or 3 dumplings and additional salt and pepper to taste.

Hearty Southwest Chili

Yield: Serves 6 to 8 | Prep Time: 15 minutes | Cook Time: 30 minutes

This is my go-to recipe for Sunday night football and tailgates. How could you ever go wrong with a combination like chili and cornbread, plus a cold beer? What I love about making chili is serving it up to a crowd. Set out a big pot along with sour cream, scallions, and cheese on the side and let your friends serve themselves, encouraging seconds and thirds until the pot's empty.

INGREDIENTS

1 pound lean ground beef

½ onion, chopped

1 green bell pepper, chopped

1 (15-ounce) can pink pinto beans, drained and rinsed

1 (15-ounce) can black beans, drained and rinsed

1 (14-ounce) can tomato sauce

1 (10-ounce) can diced tomatoes with green chiles

1 cup water, plus extra as needed

1 (1.25-ounce) packet chili seasoning

Salt

Hot sauce

Sour cream

Cornbread (page 154), crumbled

DIRECTIONS

1. Combine the ground beef, onion, and bell pepper in a large soup pot and cook over medium heat until the beef is no longer pink. Drain any fat. Add the pinto beans, black beans, tomato sauce, diced tomatoes with chiles, water, and chili seasoning. Simmer for 15 to 20 minutes. Season with salt and hot sauce to taste.

2. Serve with sour cream and cornbread.

Summer Corn Chowder

Yield: Serves 4 to 6 | Prep Time: 10 minutes | Cook Time: 30 minutes

When I think of fresh summer corn, I think of grilling—that charred taste and a big crunch when I bite into an ear of corn. This chowder is a unique twist on that same carefree summer taste of sweet, fresh corn. It's thick and creamy with hearty chunks of corn kernels.

INGREDIENTS

2 tablespoons olive oil

1 tablespoon unsalted butter

1 cup chopped yellow onion

5 cups low-sodium vegetable broth

2 baby red potatoes, quartered

4 cups frozen corn

½ cup chopped red bell pepper

½ cup chopped green bell pepper

Salt and freshly ground pepper

1 cup half-and-half

DIRECTIONS

1. In a large soup pot, heat the oil and butter over medium-high heat. Add the onion and sauté until translucent, about 10 minutes. (Do not brown the onion.) Add the broth and potatoes and bring to a boil. Reduce the heat to medium and simmer, covered, until the potatoes are tender, about 10 minutes.

2. Add the corn, bell peppers, 1 teaspoon salt, and 1 teaspoon pepper and continue to simmer over low heat for 10 minutes, stirring frequently. Remove from the heat and stir in the half-and-half. Season with additional salt and pepper to taste.

3. Ladle the soup into bowls and serve.

The Perfect Tomato Soup

Yield: Serves 4 to 6 | Prep Time: 10 minutes | Cook Time: 20 minutes

Grilled cheese and a bowl of tomato soup have the ability to melt away any troubles from a long day at work or school! Treat yourself to a fancier sandwich, like a Chicken Sandwich (page 75) along with this simple, yet delicious soup, and you'll feel right as rain in a jiffy! I use an immersion blender to smooth out this soup, but if you only have a standard blender, use that—just blend carefully in small batches.

INGREDIENTS

2 tablespoons olive oil

1 onion, chopped

4 garlic cloves, minced

2 (28-ounce) cans San Marzano plum tomatoes

1 cup low-sodium chicken broth

2 tablespoons sugar

¼ cup chopped fresh basil

1 tablespoon chopped fresh oregano

Salt and freshly ground black pepper

DIRECTIONS

1. Heat the olive oil in a large pot over medium heat. Add the onion and garlic and sauté until the onion is soft, about 5 minutes. Add the tomatoes and their juice, chicken broth, and sugar to the pot. Bring to a boil, then reduce the heat to low and simmer for 10 minutes.

2. Remove from the heat and add the basil and oregano. Using an immersion blender, puree the soup to the desired consistency. Season with salt and pepper to taste and serve.

Butternut Squash Soup

Yield: Serves 4 to 6 | Prep Time: 10 minutes | Cook Time: 20 minutes

My favorite thing about squash is its texture. When you sauté chunks of squash, they get a nice crispy coating that acts as a shield, keeping the inside soft and buttery. For this soup, I begin by sautéing the cubed squash to add this flavor shield and then purée it with flavorful ingredients to create the best squash soup you'll ever have!

INGREDIENTS

1 tablespoon olive oil

1 large butternut squash, peeled, seeded, and cut into ½-inch cubes

1 onion, diced

1 carrot, peeled and chopped

2 garlic cloves, minced

Salt and freshly ground black pepper

1 cup white wine

1 cup low-sodium vegetable broth, plus extra as needed

½ cup half-and-half, plus extra as needed

Fresh sage, for garnish (optional)

DIRECTIONS

1. Heat the oil in a large pot over medium heat. Add the squash, onion, carrot, and garlic. Season with salt and sauté until lightly browned and the squash is cooked through, 8 to 10 minutes. Add the wine and simmer until the liquid is reduced by half. Add the broth and simmer for 5 minutes.

2. Remove from the heat and add the half-and-half. Using an immersion blender, purée the soup carefully. Add more half-and-half or vegetable broth if you desire a thinner soup. Season with salt and pepper to taste and serve, garnished with fresh sage, if desired.

3

Poultry

Chicken is my go-to protein. Whether on a pizza, in
a burrito, or as the star ingredient of a dinner plate,
it is a wonderfully versatile ingredient. It's a blank canvas
that can be transformed in dozens of delicious ways, making
your weeknight dinners different every time.

Cheesy Chicken and Rice

Yield: Serves 4 | Prep Time: 5 minutes | Cook Time: 35 minutes

It's a big debate in our house: rice or pasta? I usually lose the debate, if only because the greatest pleasure I have as a chef is to make someone something they love. For my husband, the kind of dish he loves usually involves rice. This comforting, cheesy dish comes together easily, all in one pot, and the results are ooey-gooey delicious!

INGREDIENTS

1 tablespoon olive oil

1 pound chicken tenders, cut into 1-inch pieces

1 cup long-grain white rice, uncooked

1 (10.75-ounce) can cream of chicken soup

½ cup water

1 teaspoon Worcestershire sauce

½ teaspoon onion powder

½ teaspoon lemon pepper seasoning

½ teaspoon garlic powder

½ teaspoon Italian seasoning

2 cups frozen mixed vegetables

2 cups shredded cheddar cheese

DIRECTIONS

1. In a large skillet, heat the oil over medium-high heat. Add the chicken and cook until well browned, about 10 minutes. Remove the chicken and add the rice to the pan. Stir well until lightly toasted.

2. Stir in the cream of chicken soup, water, Worcestershire sauce, onion powder, lemon pepper seasoning, garlic powder, and Italian seasoning. Bring to a boil, then reduce the heat to a simmer, cover, and cook for 15 minutes.

3. Stir in the mixed vegetables and cheese. Return the chicken to the pan. Cover and cook for 5 minutes, until the chicken is warm, the cheese is melted, and the rice is tender. Let cool for about 5 minutes and serve.

Four-Ingredient OMG Chicken

Yield: Serves 2 | Prep Time: 5 minutes | Cook Time: 20 minutes

It's hard to believe that you can make something so satisfying with so few ingredients. But because of chicken's versatility and its ability to absorb flavor, all you really need are four ingredients (plus salt and pepper) to bring this dish to life. Serve this dish with Hash Brown Casserole (page 146) and your favorite veggie for a hearty meal that will please everyone at the table.

INGREDIENTS

2 boneless, skinless chicken breasts

¼ teaspoon salt

¼ teaspoon freshly ground black pepper

1 cup Caesar dressing

¼ cup crumbled feta or blue cheese

Fresh oregano

DIRECTIONS

1. Preheat the oven to 400°F. Line a baking sheet with parchment paper and place the chicken breasts on the baking sheet. Sprinkle both sides with the salt and pepper. Bake for 20 minutes.

2. Remove the chicken from the oven. Pour the Caesar dressing on top and sprinkle with the cheese and oregano. Serve.

Chicken Cordon Bleu

Yield: Serves 4 | Prep Time: 10 minutes | Cook Time: 15 minutes

Meat plus cheese: that sounds like the most indulgent culinary combination around, and take my word for it—it is! But indulgence doesn't have to be complicated. This chicken and ham combo is easy to make on any weeknight and will become everyone's favorite meal. Try serving it with Au Gratin Potatoes (page 149).

INGREDIENTS

4 (4-ounce) chicken cutlets

½ teaspoon salt

½ teaspoon freshly ground black pepper

4 thin slices deli ham

4 slices provolone cheese

¼ cup all-purpose flour

2 teaspoons olive oil

½ teaspoon unsalted butter

⅓ cup chicken broth

⅓ cup white wine

1 tablespoon lemon juice

1½ teaspoons Dijon mustard

DIRECTIONS

1. Season the chicken with the salt and pepper and top each cutlet with a slice of ham and a slice of cheese. Fold in half and secure with a toothpick.

2. Set aside 1 teaspoon flour and place the remaining flour in a shallow dish. Lightly dredge both sides of the chicken in the flour.

3. In a large skillet, heat 1 teaspoon of the olive oil and the butter over medium heat. Add 2 cutlets to the pan and cook for 2 minutes on each side. Transfer to a plate. Add the remaining oil and cook the remaining 2 cutlets. Transfer to the dish with the other cutlets.

4. Meanwhile, combine the broth, wine, lemon juice, mustard, and reserved 1 teaspoon flour in a medium bowl and whisk until smooth. Pour the broth-wine mixture into the empty pan and cook over medium heat, whisking to loosen any bits that are stuck to the skillet. Simmer for 2 minutes.

5. Return the chicken to the skillet. Cover and cook over medium heat until the cheese has melted. Spoon some sauce over each piece of chicken and serve.

Roasted Chicken

Yield: Serves 6 | Prep Time: 15 minutes | Cook Time: 1 hour

When I first started working for Thomas Keller, I'd heard about his legendary roasted chicken. At first I thought, what could be so great about roasted chicken? And then I tried his. It was amazing, and I made it my goal to learn how to roast a chicken as delectable as his. The secret is in the simplicity: Season it well; roast it hot. The skin will crisp beautifully if you make sure the chicken is dry before putting it in the oven, and it will stay juicy if you remember to baste occasionally. Serve this with Loaded Mashed Potatoes (page 153) and steamed broccoli for a complete meal.

INGREDIENTS

1 (4-pound) whole chicken, giblets discarded

1 tablespoon salt

1 tablespoon freshly ground black pepper

1 teaspoon dried oregano

DIRECTIONS

1. Preheat the oven to 450°F. Pat the chicken dry with paper towels. Season the chicken inside and out with the salt, pepper, and oregano.

2. Place the chicken breast-side up in a roasting pan or large ovenproof skillet. Roast for 50 minutes, then baste the chicken with the pan juices. Continue roasting until the chicken's juices run clear when the skin is pierced with a knife, an additional 5 to 10 minutes.

3. Let stand for 10 minutes, then carve and serve.

Crispy Chicken

Yield: Serves 4 | Prep Time: 20 minutes | Cook Time: 30 minutes

Crispy corn flakes coat these tender chicken fingers, and it's even better than you could imagine! Kids and adults will love the very slightly sweet yet savory and crunchy coating. Best of all, you'll love how easy these are to make: Prep them earlier in the day and pop them in the oven when the doorbell rings.

INGREDIENTS

4 boneless, skinless chicken breasts

1 teaspoon salt

1 teaspoon freshly ground black pepper

1 large egg

1 teaspoon water

3 cups corn flakes

2 tablespoons unsalted butter, melted

Barbecue sauce or spicy mustard for serving

DIRECTIONS

1. Preheat the oven to 400°F. Season the chicken breasts with the salt and pepper.

2. In a small bowl, whisk the egg and water together. In a medium bowl, combine the corn flakes with the melted butter. Dip each breast into the egg mixture and then roll in the cornflake mixture to coat.

3. Place the chicken on a baking sheet. Bake until no longer pink inside, about 30 minutes. Serve with barbecue sauce or spicy mustard.

Lemon-Pepper Chicken Breasts

Yield: Serves 4 | Prep Time: 20 minutes | Cook Time: 30 minutes

Lemons are bright and bold, and pack a punch. For me, they also evoke memories of warm summer days and bright sunshine. Whenever I eat this simple-to-make lemon-pepper chicken, I can almost feel the warm sun beating down on me. The tartness of the lemon becomes almost sweet as it cooks, and the pepper adds heat. Everyone in my family loves this dish, so I make it year-round. Paired with Creamed Spinach (page 157), this is a well-rounded meal.

INGREDIENTS

Marinade

6 tablespoons olive oil

1 teaspoon grated lemon zest plus 2 tablespoons juice

½ teaspoon dried oregano

¼ teaspoon kosher salt

2 tablespoons chopped fresh oregano

2 garlic cloves, grated

Chicken

1 tablespoon olive oil

4 boneless, skinless chicken breasts

Salt and freshly ground black pepper

2 lemons

DIRECTIONS

1. Preheat the oven to 375°F.

2. For the marinade: Whisk the oil, lemon zest and juice, dried oregano, and salt together to emulsify. Whisk in the fresh oregano and garlic.

3. For the chicken: Coat a large roasting pan with the olive oil. Place the chicken in the roasting pan, season it with salt and pepper, and pour the marinade on top.

4. Grate the zest from 1 lemon and set aside, then cut both lemons in half and add to the pan.

5. Roast until the chicken is fully cooked, about 30 minutes. Remove the chicken, turn the oven to broil, then return the chicken, and broil for a few minutes, until the outside is golden and slightly crisp.

6. Garnish with salt, pepper, and the reserved lemon zest and serve.

Chicken Parmesan

Yield: Serves 4 | Prep Time: 10 minutes | Cook Time: 30 minutes

Chicken Parmesan is one of those old-school dishes that is completely underrated and underappreciated. The combination of crispy bread crumbs and gooey cheese really can't be beat. Add in a fabulous marinara sauce, and you've got it made! Be sure to have extra sauce for dipping.

INGREDIENTS

4 boneless, skinless chicken breasts

2 large eggs

1 cup panko bread crumbs

1 cup freshly grated Parmesan cheese

1 cup marinara sauce, warmed, plus extra for serving

Oregano for garnish

DIRECTIONS

1. Preheat the oven to 400°F. Line a baking sheet with parchment paper.

2. Pound the chicken breasts with a meat mallet to ½-inch thickness.

3. In a small bowl, crack both eggs and beat until smooth. Combine the panko and Parmesan cheese in a zip-top plastic bag. Dredge the chicken breasts into the egg mixture, followed by the panko mixture. Shake off any excess crumbs and lay on the baking sheet.

4. Bake until the chicken is golden and fully cooked, about 30 minutes. Spoon the marinara over the chicken. Garnish with oregano and serve with extra marinara on the side.

Bourbon Chicken

Yield: Serves 4 | Prep Time: 10 minutes | Cook Time: 20 minutes

When I say "bourbon" at home, ears perk up. And when it has to do with a weeknight dinner, interest in that meal goes from a five to a ten with that one word. The smoky, savory flavor from a favorite happy hour drink has found its way to our traditional Tuesday chicken dinners. Smoky Baked Beans (page 158) go well with the rough-and-tumble flavor of this chicken dish.

INGREDIENTS

1 cup bourbon

1 cup maple syrup

¼ cup lemon juice

4 boneless, skinless chicken breasts

Salt and freshly ground black pepper

2 tablespoons olive oil

DIRECTIONS

1. Preheat the oven to 400°F.

2. In a small saucepan, combine the bourbon, maple syrup, and lemon juice. Simmer over medium heat for 5 minutes until the sauce has slightly thickened.

3. Season the chicken breasts with salt and pepper. In a medium ovensafe skillet, heat the oil over medium heat, add the chicken, and pour the bourbon-maple mixture on top. Place the skillet in the oven and cook for 20 minutes, until the chicken is done. Serve.

Chicken Sandwiches

Yield: Serves 2 | Prep Time: 10 minutes | Cook Time: 20 minutes

I am on the search for the perfect chicken sandwich, and the conclusion I've come to is that simple is better. I like pairing these with Fried Pickles (page 30) for a little extra crunch!

INGREDIENTS

2 boneless, skinless chicken breasts

Salt and freshly ground black pepper

¼ teaspoon Italian seasoning

2 hamburger buns

1 tablespoon unsalted butter, softened

¼ cup mayonnaise

1 cup mixed green lettuce

1 tomato, sliced

DIRECTIONS

1. Preheat the oven to 400°F. Line a baking sheet with parchment paper.

2. Season the chicken breasts with salt, pepper, and Italian seasoning and place on the prepared baking sheet. Cook until the chicken is no longer pink inside, about 20 minutes.

3. Meanwhile, spread the cut sides of each bun with the butter. Place the buns on the oven rack buttered side up and toast them lightly.

4. Top each bun with mayonnaise, lettuce, and tomato. Add the chicken breasts and serve.

Turkey Wrap

Yield: Makes 1 wrap | Prep Time: 5 minutes | Cook Time: n/a

I love making sandwiches with wraps, not because I think they're a healthier option than bread, but because of the accomplishment I feel when I see the pretty spirals of color after they're assembled and sliced. It's like pitching a tent or finding your destination without using a map. Doesn't seem complicated, but you *know* when it's done right. Serve this one with the Olive and Mozzarella Antipasti (page 9) for a complete meal.

INGREDIENTS

Dipping Sauce

½ cup mayonnaise

2 tablespoons Sriracha sauce

1 teaspoon lime juice

¼ teaspoon salt

¼ teaspoon freshly ground black pepper

Wrap

2 tablespoons Dijon mustard

2 tablespoons mayonnaise

1 large wrap or tortilla

1 tomato, thinly sliced

Romaine lettuce

2 slices provolone cheese

3 slices turkey

DIRECTIONS

1. For the dipping sauce: Stir all the ingredients together in a small bowl and set aside.

2. For the wrap: Spread the mustard and mayonnaise on the wrap. Top with the tomato, lettuce, cheese, and turkey. Roll the wrap tightly and slice in half or into 1-inch rounds. Serve with the dipping sauce.

General Tso's Chicken

Yield: Serves 4 to 6 | Prep Time: 15 minutes | Cook Time: 4½ hours on low, then 20 minutes on high; non-active

No one is sure of the origin of this popular recipe, but I know you will love this easy weeknight version. The best part is that all the hard work is done for you, thanks to the slow cooker. Serve with rice and some roasted broccoli for a complete meal.

INGREDIENTS

2½ pounds boneless, skinless chicken breasts, cut into 1½-inch pieces

½ cup plus 2 tablespoons chicken broth

½ cup packed light brown sugar

3 tablespoons hoisin sauce

3 tablespoons ketchup

2 tablespoons soy sauce

1 teaspoon finely minced ginger

1 teaspoon finely minced garlic

1 teaspoon Sriracha sauce

½ teaspoon red pepper flakes

¼ teaspoon sesame oil

1 tablespoon cornstarch

¼ cup peanuts, halved

Scallions, sliced thin

DIRECTIONS

1. Coat the inside of a 6-quart slow cooker with cooking spray.

2. Combine the chicken, ½ cup of the broth, the sugar, hoisin sauce, ketchup, soy sauce, ginger, garlic, Sriracha sauce, red pepper flakes, and oil in a medium bowl; stir to mix well. Place in the prepared slow cooker, cover, and cook for 4½ hours on low.

3. Stir the cornstarch and remaining 2 tablespoons broth in a small bowl until smooth. Stir into the chicken mixture with the peanuts, cover, and continue to cook for another 20 minutes on high, or until the sauce thickens.

4. Sprinkle with sliced scallions and serve.

Orange Chicken

Yield: Serves 4 | Prep Time: 15 minutes | Cook Time: 15 minutes

Orange chicken is a popular choice on takeout menus—and for good reason. The flavorful sauce coating the crunchy chicken is sticky, zesty, and sometimes quite spicy. This recipe combines the crunchy, lightly fried chicken with a zesty sauce that the whole family will love. Serve with rice and steamed veggies.

INGREDIENTS

5 large egg whites

2 tablespoons plus 1 teaspoon cornstarch

1½ pounds boneless, skinless chicken breasts, cut into 1-inch pieces

½ cup orange juice

1 tablespoon soy sauce

1 tablespoon packed light brown sugar

1 tablespoon rice wine vinegar

¼ teaspoon sesame oil

¼ teaspoon salt

1 garlic clove, minced

Vegetable oil

Chopped scallions

DIRECTIONS

1. In a large bowl, combine the egg whites and 2 tablespoons of the cornstarch with a fork. Add the chicken to the mixture and let sit for 10 minutes.

2. Meanwhile, combine the orange juice, soy sauce, sugar, vinegar, sesame oil, salt, and garlic in a small nonstick skillet and stir well. Heat over medium-high heat, until bubbling and starting to thicken, about 5 minutes.

3. Whisk together the remaining 1 teaspoon cornstarch and ¼ cup water in a small bowl. Whisk 1 to 2 tablespoons of the cornstarch slurry into the sauce and cook until thickened, about 1 minute.

4. Pour enough oil into a Dutch oven to reach a depth of 2 inches and heat to 350°F. Carefully drop the chicken into the oil and move it around to break up any clumps. Cook for 3 to 4 minutes.

5. Remove and let the pieces drain on a paper towel–lined plate for 2 to 3 minutes.

6. Toss the chicken in the sauce, sprinkle with scallions, and serve.

Easy Chicken Fried Rice

Yield: Serves 6 to 8 | Prep Time: 15 minutes | Cook Time: 10 minutes

Fried rice is one of those dishes that can be thrown together in a hurry after a late afternoon of kids' sports and activities. Earlier in the week, cook extra rice when you are making dinner and stash the leftovers. Frozen vegetables and rotisserie chicken make this hearty enough for a complete meal.

INGREDIENTS

1 teaspoon olive oil

1½ cups precooked chicken, such as rotisserie-style, diced

3 cups cooked rice, cold

1 (16-ounce) bag frozen mixed vegetables

¼ cup low-sodium soy sauce

3 tablespoons rice wine vinegar

2 large eggs

Salt and freshly ground black pepper

DIRECTIONS

1. In a wok or large nonstick skillet, heat the oil over high heat. Add the chicken, rice, and frozen vegetables and cook, stirring constantly, until warmed through, about 5 minutes.

2. Add the soy sauce and vinegar, stirring to combine well. Push all the food to the sides, leaving a clear space in the middle of the pan. Crack the eggs into the space and immediately stir. Once the eggs are cooked, stir everything together, season with salt and pepper, and serve.

4

Beef and Pork

I grew up on my family's farm in Minnesota and learned at a
young age to appreciate the flavor beef and pork bring to all types
of dishes. The recipes in this chapter celebrate these versatile
flavors and will satisfy any adult and excite any kid around.

Daniel's Meatloaf

Yield: Serves 6 | Prep Time: 15 minutes | Cook Time: 1 hour

My first American kitchen job was with Daniel Boulud, one of the most celebrated chefs alive. He is as kind as he is talented, and he was a fantastic mentor to me. One of his jobs was to make the weekly family-style meal for his staff, and he always made meatloaf. At the time I thought it was because it's a simple dish to make when your prep list is long, but he truly loved his recipe. He made it our restaurant family's tradition, and this recipe is inspired by his. A fresh veggie side and Loaded Mashed Potatoes (page 153) were likely to appear on the table at these family-style meals.

INGREDIENTS

2 pounds lean ground beef

½ cup Italian-style bread crumbs

1 large egg

1 teaspoon salt

1 teaspoon freshly ground black pepper

1 teaspoon onion powder

½ teaspoon garlic powder

1 cup ketchup

DIRECTIONS

1. Preheat the oven to 350°F.

2. Place the beef, bread crumbs, egg, salt, pepper, onion powder, and garlic powder in a large bowl and mix well. Transfer to a loaf pan. Spread the ketchup over the top. Bake for 55 minutes to 1 hour, or until a meat thermometer reaches 160°F. Let cool for 5 minutes, then slice into 1-inch thick slices with a serrated knife and serve.

Pot Roast

Yield: Serves 6 | Prep Time: 15 minutes | Cook Time: 3 hours

Pot roast is a braised beef dish, one that has two steps, both equally important. You must first brown your beef before partially submerging it in liquid to cook. The browning induces a Maillard reaction, adding that meaty savor, and when covered, the beef cooks slowly to create a tender piece of meat for a group to share. Loaded Mashed Potatoes (page 153) make the perfect accompaniment to this wonderful roast.

INGREDIENTS

1 (4-to 5-pound) chuck roast

1 tablespoon salt

1 tablespoon freshly ground black pepper

3 tablespoons olive oil

3 cups baby carrots

1 cup beef broth

3 sprigs fresh thyme

DIRECTIONS

1. Preheat the oven to 275°F. Season the roast with the salt and pepper

2. Heat the oil in a Dutch oven over medium-high heat. Add the carrots and cook until slightly browned, about 1 minute. Add the roast and sear for 1 minute on all sides until it is nice and brown all over, then transfer the roast to a plate.

3. Add the broth to the pot and stir, scraping the bottom with a wooden spoon to bring the flavor up. Return the roast to the pot and add the thyme sprigs.

4. Cover the pot, transfer to the oven, and roast for 3 hours. Transfer the roast to a carving board and slice it thinly. Arrange the slices on a serving platter with the carrots. Spoon the pan juices over the meat and serve.

Stuffed Peppers

Yield: Serves 2 to 4 | Prep Time: 15 minutes | Cook Time: 40 minutes

I love eating something in a vessel that can then itself be eaten, like a bread bowl or an ice cream cone. This is a fun all-in-one meal that can be sliced up and devoured without leaving a trace, or extra dishes, behind. Simply sauté, stuff, bake, and eat!

INGREDIENTS

1 pound lean ground beef

½ cup chopped onion

1 (14.5-ounce) can diced tomatoes in juice

1 (8-ounce) can whole kernel corn

2½ cups stuffing mix

¼ cup chopped fresh cilantro

1 teaspoon salt

2 bell peppers, any color

1 tablespoon unsalted butter

¼ cup grated Parmesan cheese

DIRECTIONS

1. Preheat the oven to 400°F. Lightly coat an 8 X 8-inch baking dish with cooking spray.

2. In a large skillet, cook the beef over medium-high heat for 5 minutes, stirring to break up clumps. Add the onion and cook, stirring, for 2 minutes until the onion is translucent. Drain the meat mixture and return the pan to the heat. Add the tomatoes, corn, 2 cups of the stuffing mix, the cilantro, and salt and stir well.

3. While the meat is cooking, cut the bell peppers in half lengthwise. Remove the top, seeds, and all of the white membrane. Arrange in the prepared baking dish. Lightly pack the filling into the peppers.

4. Melt the butter in a small bowl in the microwave and add the remaining ½ cup stuffing mix and half of the cheese, stirring to coat the bread. Spoon on top of the filled peppers, then sprinkle with the remaining cheese. Add ¼ cup water to the bottom of the baking dish and cover with foil.

5. Bake for 25 to 30 minutes, until the peppers are just tender but not collapsing. Serve immediately.

Bacon Cheeseburger Walking Tacos

Yield: Serves 6 | Prep Time: 10 minutes | Cook Time: 2 to 3 hours, non-active

Rushing home from school, only to head out to football or basketball games, kids often need something to grab and go. Toss these ingredients in the slow cooker in the afternoon, put the bags of Fritos on the counter next to the slow cooker, and the kids will know exactly what to do.

INGREDIENTS

1 pound lean ground beef, browned and drained

1 (10-ounce) can tomatoes with chiles

2 cups shredded four-cheese blend, plus extra for serving

1 (8-ounce) package cream cheese, softened

6 slices bacon, cooked and crumbled

3 tablespoons chopped fresh parsley

1 tablespoon Worcestershire sauce

6 snack-sized bags Fritos

DIRECTIONS

1. Place the browned beef, tomatoes, shredded cheese, cream cheese, bacon, parsley, and Worcestershire sauce in a 6-quart slow cooker. Stir well. Cook for 2 to 3 hours on low until the cheese has melted.

2. Let cool slightly. Open the bags of Fritos, scoop about ½ cup of the beef mixture into each bag, and top with additional cheese. Eat immediately.

Slow Cooker Pulled Pork

Yield: Serves 8 | Prep Time: 5 minutes | Cook Time: 10 hours, non-active

This is perfect for a summer get-together, or any night of the week, because you can go about your day while the pork cooks and you won't heat up the house. The slow cooker creates tender, juicy pork with little effort. Here, the pork is paired with corn tortillas and salsa for a uniquely festive meal, but you could also serve it on crusty rolls with coleslaw for a great weeknight dinner.

INGREDIENTS

3 to 4 pounds boneless pork loin roast

Salt and freshly ground black pepper

1 small onion, sliced

1 (12-ounce) can Dr Pepper or other dark cola

1¼ cups barbeque sauce, plus extra as needed

Corn tortillas

1 (15.2-ounce) can whole kernel corn, drained, rinsed, and warmed

1 jar salsa

DIRECTIONS

1. Season the pork generously with salt and pepper. Spread the onion slices in the bottom of a 6-quart slow cooker and set the pork on top. Pour the can of Dr Pepper over the pork. Cover and cook for 10 hours on low.

2. Remove the pork from the slow cooker and shred with 2 forks. Return to the slow cooker. (You may need to pour off some extra liquid.) Add the barbecue sauce and mix well. Cook for 10 to 15 minutes on high to bring the flavors together. Adjust the consistency with extra barbeque sauce if desired. Serve on corn tortillas with the corn and salsa.

Pork Chops in Mushroom Sauce

Yield: Serves 4 | Prep Time: 5 minutes | Cook Time: 30 minutes

Hearty, meaty mushrooms are smothered in sauce to perfectly complement seared pork chops. A great meal for kids and sophisticated enough for adults, this has become one of my favorites after a busy day. Everyone will love Au Gratin Potatoes (page 149) paired with this hearty dish.

INGREDIENTS

1 cup all-purpose flour

2 tablespoons onion powder

1 teaspoon smoked paprika

1 teaspoon salt

½ teaspoon freshly ground black pepper

4 bone-in pork chops, ¾ inch thick

2 tablespoons olive oil

1 cup chicken broth

8 ounces white mushrooms, trimmed and sliced

½ cup buttermilk

DIRECTIONS

1. Place the flour, onion powder, paprika, salt, and pepper in a zip-top plastic bag and shake vigorously to mix. Drop in the pork chops one at a time and shake so that the flour mixture adheres in an even layer.

2. In a large, deep skillet (big enough to hold all of the chops at one time), heat 1 tablespoon of the oil over medium-high heat until just smoking. Shake off any excess flour from the chops and add them to the pan, reserving the flour mixture. Fry for 5 minutes on each side until golden brown, then remove to a plate (the chops may not be fully cooked).

3. Add the remaining 1 tablespoon oil and 1 tablespoon of the reserved flour mixture to the pan and stir briskly with a whisk for 1 minute until the flour cooks and smells toasty. Add the broth and whisk for 4 to 5 minutes until thickened. Add the mushrooms and cook for 2 to 3 minutes.

4. Whisk in the buttermilk, cooking and stirring for a few minutes until thickened. Lower the heat to medium-low, return the chops to the skillet, spoon some of the sauce over them, and simmer for 10 minutes, spooning the sauce over the chops from time to time. Serve the chops with the sauce.

Ranch Pork Chops

Yield: Serves 6 | Prep Time: 5 minutes | Cook Time: 4 hours, non-active

After a day of running errands, taking the kids to and fro, or a long work day, the last thing you want to think about is what to make for dinner. This dish is made with pantry staples, so you'll be able to whip it up in the morning whenever you're in a rush but still want something flavorful and comforting for dinner. Cook up some Cornbread (page 154) when you get home; it'll soak up the gravy on everyone's plate.

INGREDIENTS

6 (5-ounce) boneless pork chops

1 (1-ounce) packet ranch dressing and seasoning mix

2 (10.75-ounce) cans cream of mushroom soup

DIRECTIONS

1. Spray the insert of a 6-quart slow cooker with cooking spray.

2. Place the pork chops into the slow cooker. Sprinkle half of the ranch seasoning over the chops. Cover the chops with the soup. Sprinkle the remaining ranch seasoning on top. Cover and cook for 4 hours on high. Serve.

Sticky Ribs

Yield: Serves 4 | Prep Time: 5 minutes plus 2 hours marinade time | Cook Time: 6 hours, non-active

I don't make ribs very often, but when I do I always say, "I should make these more often." What I like about the smoky meat is that it's interactive. You have to work a little for that tender meat to fall off the bone, and sticky hands are evidence that you were successful. The marinade on these ribs features Asian flavors like citrus, hoisin, and chili sauce and couldn't be easier to make. Served with smoky Smoky Baked Beans (page 158), this is a meal everyone will request over and over again.

INGREDIENTS

Grated zest and juice of 1 large orange

½ cup soy sauce

½ cup hoisin sauce

¼ cup honey

¼ cup bottled sweet chili sauce

3 tablespoons rice wine vinegar

2 tablespoons sesame oil

1 tablespoon finely minced fresh garlic

4–5 pounds baby back ribs, ends of ribs trimmed

2 tablespoons cornstarch

2 tablespoons water

DIRECTIONS

1. Place the orange zest and juice, soy sauce, hoisin sauce, honey, chili sauce, vinegar, oil, and garlic in a large zip-top plastic bag and mix well. Add the ribs, seal the bag, and squeeze and rub through the sealed bag to coat all of the meat with the sauce. Refrigerate for at least 2 hours, or up to overnight.

2. Spray the insert of a 6-quart slow cooker with cooking spray and place the ribs and their marinade in the cooker. Cook for 6 hours on low.

3. Remove the ribs to a warm platter and transfer the marinade to a small saucepan. Bring to a simmer over medium heat. In a small bowl, combine the cornstarch and water to make a smooth paste and stir into the simmering liquid, stirring occasionally until the sauce thickens. Pour the sauce over the ribs and serve.

Smothered Pork Chops

Yield: Serves 6 | Prep Time: 10 minutes | Cook Time: 20 to 25 minutes

Rich gravy with juicy pork chops make a perfect dinner. The crisp flour coating allows all the pork's juices to stay inside, which I absolutely love.

INGREDIENTS

¼ cup all-purpose flour

1 teaspoon salt

1 teaspoon freshly ground black pepper

1 large egg, beaten

2 tablespoons water

1½ cups seasoned bread crumbs

6 boneless pork chops, ¾-inch thick

1 (10.5-ounce) jar turkey gravy

Fresh thyme, for garnish

DIRECTIONS

1. Preheat the oven to 400°F. Lightly coat a baking sheet with cooking spray.

2. In a large zip-top plastic bag, combine the flour, salt, and pepper. Combine the beaten egg and water in a shallow dish. Place the bread crumbs in another shallow dish.

3. Add a pork chop to the bag with the flour. Shake the bag, remove the chop, and tap off any excess flour. Dip the pork chop in the egg mixture, then in the bread crumbs. Place on the baking sheet. Repeat with the remaining chops. Bake until the chops are lightly browned and cooked through, 20 to 25 minutes.

4. Pour the gravy into a microwave-safe bowl and microwave until hot for 1 to 2 minutes. Serve the gravy with the pork chops and garnish with the fresh thyme.

Kielbasa, Pepper, and Onion Hash

Yield: Serves 6 | Prep Time: 15 minutes | Cook Time: 15 to 20 minutes

I enjoy this versatile dish at pretty much any time of day. Topping it with a fried egg adds protein and gives it a rich taste, making it suitable even for breakfast. Try it for a weeknight dinner and then have leftovers for Sunday brunch.

INGREDIENTS

3 tablespoons olive oil

3 small or 2 large potatoes, peeled and diced

Salt and freshly ground black pepper

1 (14-ounce) package smoked kielbasa or turkey kielbasa, cut into ¼-inch rounds

1 green bell pepper, diced

½ yellow, red, or orange bell pepper, diced

1 onion, diced

6 large eggs (optional)

½ teaspoon herbs de Provence

¼ teaspoon red pepper flakes

Thyme sprigs, for garnish (optional)

DIRECTIONS

1. In a large skillet, heat 2 tablespoons of the oil over medium-high heat. Add the potatoes and cook until golden and cooked through, about 10 minutes. Season with salt and pepper and set aside.

2. Meanwhile, in another skillet, heat the remaining tablespoon oil over medium heat. Brown the kielbasa for 5 minutes. Transfer the kielbasa to a large serving bowl. Add the bell peppers and onion to the empty skillet and cook until they are softened, about 5 minutes. Season with salt and pepper. Add to the bowl with the kielbasa.

3. If you're including fried eggs, return the skillet to the heat until the remaining fat is hot. Lower the heat to low and crack an egg over the skillet. Cook for one minute or until the egg white is no longer translucent. Transfer to a plate lined with paper towels. Repeat with each egg.

4. Add the cooked potatoes to the bowl. Season with the herbs de Provence and red pepper flakes and mix together.

5. Serve, topping each serving with a fried egg and fresh thyme, if desired.

Bacon and Cheddar Quiche

Yield: Serves 6 | Prep Time: 20 minutes | Cook Time: 1 hour

When I was on The Food Network for the second time, I was tasked with making quiche. Chef Richard Blais was the judge of this competition, and despite the many challenges I faced on the show, I made it and he liked it! This is my go-to recipe: easy enough to make in the heat of competition but sophisticated enough to present to guests around your dinner table.

INGREDIENTS

1 (9-inch) pie crust

4 large eggs

1 cup half-and-half

½ teaspoon salt

½ teaspoon freshly ground black pepper

3 scallions, thinly sliced

6 slices bacon, cooked and crumbled

1 cup shredded cheddar cheese

1 cup finely chopped onion

Thyme sprigs, for garnish

DIRECTIONS

1. Preheat the oven to 325°F. Bake the pie crust for 15 minutes, until lightly browned. Meanwhile, in a medium bowl, beat the eggs lightly, then whisk in the half-and-half, salt, pepper, and scallions. Sprinkle the bacon, cheese, and onion into the baked pie crust and add the egg mixture.

2. Bake the quiche for 45 to 50 minutes, or until a knife inserted in the center comes out clean. Let stand for 10 minutes, then serve, garnished with the thyme.

Philly Cheesesteak Sandwiches

Yield: Serves 4 | Prep Time: 10 minutes | Cook Time: 20 minutes

Of all the cheesesteaks I've tried in my life, my very favorite is in my hometown. The little mom-and-pop diner on the corner piles their sandwiches high with the most delectable combination of juicy meat and gooey cheese. I'll never forget it. This recipe comes pretty close. Make it for your friends and family, and they will be asking for it again and again.

INGREDIENTS

2–2½ pounds strip loin, trimmed and cut into strips

1 tablespoon olive oil

1 teaspoon salt

1 teaspoon freshly ground black pepper

1 onion, sliced

1 red bell pepper, sliced

4 slices provolone cheese

4 hoagie rolls

DIRECTIONS

1. Heat a griddle or grill pan over high heat. Brush the steak strips with the oil and season with the salt and pepper. Cook for 45 to 60 seconds on each side.

2. Add the onion and bell pepper. Cook, moving with tongs, until soft and charred, about 10 minutes.

3. Add a slice of cheese to the bottom half of each roll. Top with 4 to 6 strips of steak and some onion and pepper slices, and serve.

Reuben Panini

Yield: Serves 4 | Prep Time: 5 minutes | Cook Time: 30 minutes

I remember going to the local deli with my grandfather when I was a kid. We always ordered Reubens. It was an odd choice for a small child, but while most of my friends wanted PB&J or grilled cheese, I loved the tangy sauerkraut and rich beef. Make these in the evening in a panini press and devour with chips.

INGREDIENTS

4 tablespoons unsalted butter

8 slices marbled rye bread

1 cup Thousand Island dressing

8 slices Swiss cheese

16 slices deli corned beef

1 cup sauerkraut

DIRECTIONS

1. Preheat a panini press on medium heat.

2. Lightly butter one side of each bread slice. Spread the unbuttered sides with Thousand Island dressing. On the dressing side of 4 slices of bread, layer 1 slice cheese, 4 slices corned beef, ¼ cup sauerkraut and 1 more slice of cheese. Top with the remaining bread slices, buttered side up.

3. Place the sandwiches on the press and cook until both sides are golden brown, about 15 minutes per side. Serve hot.

Meatball Sandwiches

Yield: Serves 6 to 8 | Prep Time: 25 minutes | Cook Time: 35 to 40 minutes

I like to make a few of these generous sandwiches whenever my husband has friends over to watch a football game. They are hearty, everyone loves them, and they go great with a beer or two. If you really want to cut the cooking time down, don't hesitate to use prepared frozen meatballs. I use them all the time, but sometimes if guests are coming, I like to make them from scratch.

INGREDIENTS

1 Barbecue Meatballs recipe (see page 6)

1 (½-pound) block provolone cheese

6 hoagie rolls

DIRECTIONS

1. Make the Barbecue Meatballs recipe. Take the block of provolone cheese and use a cheese grater to shred until you have about 1½ cups of cheese. Toast the hoagie rolls.

2. Spoon the meatballs on the bottom half of the hoagie roll and top with a sprinkling of shredded cheese and the top half of the bun. Serve.

Ham and Cheese Potatoes

Yield: Serves 4 to 6 | Prep Time: 10 minutes | Cook Time: 45 minutes

Whenever I eat ham and cheese potatoes, I am instantly comforted. A little pork, a lot of cheese, and a dash of spice is a great way to dress up potatoes. What I love about this dish is that it is appropriate any time of day, not just dinner. Heat leftovers up the next morning for a hearty breakfast!

INGREDIENTS

1 (32-ounce) bag frozen potatoes O'Brien

1 (5-ounce) ham steak, cubed

2 cups shredded cheddar cheese

1 teaspoon salt

1 teaspoon freshly ground black pepper

1 teaspoon cayenne pepper

DIRECTIONS

1. Preheat the oven to 400°F. Coat a 9 x 13-inch baking dish with cooking spray.

2. Combine all of the ingredients in the baking dish and stir. Bake for 30 minutes, stir, and bake for another 15 minutes. Serve.

Asian Burgers

Yield: Serves 4 | Prep Time: 15 minutes | Cook Time: 10 minutes

Burgers are a quick go-to on a busy weeknight; this version adds a fun international twist with a slightly spicy Asian flavor from the chili and hoisin sauces. The burgers are topped with a spicy slaw for a sandwich that everyone will love.

INGREDIENTS

1 pound lean ground beef

½ cup panko bread crumbs

¼ red onion, finely chopped

1 large egg

1 tablespoon soy sauce

1 tablespoon hoisin sauce

2 teaspoons Asian chili sauce

1 teaspoon salt

1 teaspoon garlic powder

½ teaspoon ground ginger

2 cups coleslaw

2 teaspoons Sriracha sauce

4 hamburger buns

DIRECTIONS

1. Preheat the grill to medium-high heat (about 450°F).

2. In a large bowl, mix the beef, panko, onion, egg, soy sauce, hoisin sauce, chili sauce, salt, garlic powder, and ginger until well combined. Form the mixture into 4 patties. Place on the grill and cook for 3 to 4 minutes on each side, for medium. Remove from the grill and let rest for 5 minutes.

3. Meanwhile, mix the coleslaw with the Sriracha sauce and set aside.

4. Serve each burger on a bun with spicy slaw.

NOTES

If you do not have a grill, heat about 2 tablespoons olive oil in a grill pan or large skillet over high heat. Place the burgers in the pan and cook as directed.

Beef Stroganoff

Yield: Serves 4 | Prep Time: 15 minutes | Cook Time: 35 minutes

A classic Russian cookbook, *A Gift to Young Housewives* by Elena Molokhovets, provided possibly the first version of this beef dish, a staple for a young person learning to feed a family. Over the years the recipe has changed, but the sentiment of that original publication has stuck with me, and when I make this dish for dinner, I feel it's a gesture of love, from wife to husband, daughter to mother, friend to friend.

INGREDIENTS

8 ounces egg noodles

2 tablespoons unsalted butter

8 ounces white mushrooms, trimmed and chopped

1 onion, thinly sliced

2 pounds beef sirloin steak, cubed

1½ cups beef broth

1 teaspoon salt

1 teaspoon Worcestershire sauce

¼ cup all-purpose flour

1½ cups sour cream

DIRECTIONS

1. Bring a large pot of water to a boil. Add the egg noodles and salt and cook until al dente. Drain and return the pasta to the pot. Set aside.

2. In a large skillet, melt the butter over medium heat, add the mushrooms and onion, and cook, stirring occasionally, until the onion is tender.

3. Add the beef and cook until brown. Stir in 1 cup of the broth, the salt, and the Worcestershire sauce. Bring to a boil, then reduce the heat, cover, and simmer for 15 minutes.

4. In a small bowl whisk the remaining ½ cup broth and the flour together and add to the beef mixture. Heat to boiling, stirring constantly, and boil for 1 minute. Let cool for 2 minutes and stir in the sour cream. Serve over the noodles.

5

Pasta and Vegetarian

Angel hair, elbows, spirals, shells! So many pasta shapes to choose from, and so many ways to prepare them. This chapter is full of dinner ideas that feature this favorite carb, plus some bonus recipes for all you vegetable enthusiasts out there.

Tuna Casserole

Yield: Serves 6 | Prep Time: 20 minutes | Cook Time: 40 minutes

I love the way that tuna, when combined with a white sauce or mayonnaise, is slightly sweet and salty, perfectly complementing the noodles that add to that delicious bite.

INGREDIENTS

4 cups wide egg noodles

Salt

2 (10.75-ounce) cans cream of mushroom soup

1 cup whole milk

1½ pounds canned chunk tuna, well drained

2 cups peas, thawed if frozen

2 tablespoons canned pimentos, drained

¼ teaspoon freshly ground black pepper

DIRECTIONS

1. Preheat the oven to 400°F. Lightly coat a 9 x 13-inch baking dish with cooking spray.

2. Bring a large pot of water to a boil. Add the egg noodles and salt to taste and cook until al dente. Drain and reserve.

3. While the noodles cook, combine the soup and milk in a large bowl and stir well. Add the tuna, peas, pimentos, and pepper and stir to combine. Add the drained noodles and stir. Pour into the prepared baking dish.

4. Bake until bubbling and the top is golden brown, about 30 minutes. Let cool slightly and serve.

Eggplant Parmesan

Yield: Serves 10 | Prep Time: 1 hour 10 minutes | Cook Time: 1 hour 15 minutes

Eggplants hold not only a lot of nutrients, but also a lot of flavor! This may be hard to believe, but their juicy flesh has a unique taste that combines well with rich flavors.

INGREDIENTS

Eggplant

2 (1-pound) eggplants, cut into ½-inch-thick slices

Kosher salt

2 large eggs, beaten

2 cups panko bread crumbs

¼ cup grated Parmesan cheese

Filling

1 (15-ounce) container part-skim ricotta cheese

½ cup torn basil leaves

¼ cup grated Parmesan cheese

1 large egg, lightly beaten

1½ teaspoons minced garlic

½ teaspoon red pepper flakes

¼ teaspoon kosher salt

For Layering

1 (24-ounce) jar pasta sauce

¼ teaspoon kosher salt

8 ounces fresh mozzarella cheese, sliced

¾ cup shredded provolone cheese

DIRECTIONS

1. For the eggplant: Place the eggplant slices on a paper towel–lined baking sheet. Liberally sprinkle the slices with kosher salt and let sit for 45 minutes. The eggplant will release its bitter liquid. Rinse the salt off of the eggplant slices and pat dry thoroughly.

2. Preheat the oven to 375°F.

3. Combine the eggs and 1 tablespoon water in a shallow dish. Combine the panko and Parmesan in another shallow dish.

4. Dip the eggplant slices in the egg mixture, then the panko mixture. Place 1 inch apart on a baking sheet. Spray each slice lightly with cooking spray. Bake for 15 minutes, flip the eggplant over and bake for an additional 15 minutes, until golden.

5. To make the filling: While the eggplant is baking, combine the first 7 ingredients in a medium bowl.

6. Lightly coat a 9 x 13-inch baking dish with cooking spray. Spoon ½ cup pasta sauce in the bottom of the baking dish. Layer half of the eggplant over the sauce and sprinkle with 1/8 teaspoon kosher salt. Top with ¾ cup sauce. Spread half of the ricotta mixture over the sauce and top with one-third of the mozzarella and one-quarter of the provolone. Arrange the remaining eggplant over the cheese, sprinkle with the remaining salt, and top with ¾ cup sauce. Spread the remaining ricotta over the sauce and top with half of the remaining mozzarella and one-third of the remaining provolone. Spread 1 cup sauce over the top.

7. Cover with foil and bake for 35 minutes. Remove the foil and top with the remaining mozzarella and provolone. Bake for 10 minutes until the cheeses are melted. Serve.

VARIATIONS

Experiment with different cheeses in the filling, such as fontina, Italian blend, or cream cheese.

Baked Ziti

Yield: Serves 8 | Prep Time: 20 minutes | Cook Time: 45 minutes

Baked ziti is one of those dishes that is perfect for so many occasions. It holds incredibly well, so you can take this to a potluck, over to a friend's house, or even make it ahead on the weekend when you might have an extra bit of time. This recipe is foolproof, full of both flavor and shortcuts.

INGREDIENTS

8 ounces ziti

1 tablespoon olive oil

8 ounces lean ground beef

½ cup chopped onion

1 teaspoon Italian seasoning

½ teaspoon garlic powder

Salt and freshly ground black pepper

1 (24-ounce) jar marinara sauce

½ cup ricotta cheese

4 ounces sliced fresh mozzarella cheese

DIRECTIONS

1. Preheat the oven to 350°F. Lightly spray a 9 × 13-inch baking dish with cooking spray.

2. Bring a large pot of water to a boil. Add the pasta and cook until al dente. Drain and set aside.

3. Meanwhile, heat the oil in a large skillet over medium-high heat, add the beef, and cook until mostly browned. Add the onion, Italian seasoning, garlic powder, and salt and pepper to taste and cook until the meat is cooked through, about 5 minutes. Add the marinara sauce, bring to a low simmer, and cook for 5 minutes. Add the pasta and stir until thoroughly combined.

4. Pour half of the pasta mixture into the prepared dish and spread evenly. Top with dollops of ricotta and spread lightly. Top with the remaining pasta mixture. Cover with the mozzarella and bake for 15 to 20 minutes, until bubbling and cheese is melted and lightly golden. Let cool slightly and serve.

VARIATIONS

Try sausage, ground turkey, or even pepperoni in place of the ground beef.

Weeknight Turkey Lasagna

Yield: Serves 6 to 8 | Prep Time: 15 minutes | Cook Time: 1 hour

My grandmother's lasagna recipe takes all day to make, because she labors over the stove, making the most delicious tomato and meat sauce. During the week, I've found that I can take a few simple shortcuts to make a mouthwatering meal that tastes just as wonderful as Grandma's. It's hearty and warm, filled with gooey cheese and plenty of sauce. If you have time, double the recipe and freeze the second portion for up to a month; it reheats amazingly well!

INGREDIENTS

2 tablespoons olive oil

1 onion, chopped

3 garlic cloves, minced

1 pound ground turkey

Salt and freshly ground black pepper

1 (24-ounce) jar marinara sauce

8 ounces lasagna noodles

1 (15-ounce) container ricotta cheese

1 cup grated Parmesan cheese, plus ¼ cup for sprinkling

1 large egg, lightly beaten

2 cups shredded mozzarella cheese

¾ cup chopped fresh basil

DIRECTIONS

1. Preheat the oven to 400°F.

2. In a large skillet, heat the oil over medium-low heat. Add the onion and cook for 5 minutes, until translucent. Add the garlic and cook until fragrant but not brown. Add the turkey and cook, breaking it up with a fork, for 8 to 10 minutes, or until no longer pink. Season the meat with salt and pepper. Stir in the jar of marinara sauce and simmer for 15 to 20 minutes.

3. Meanwhile, fill a large bowl with hot tap water. Add the lasagna noodles and allow them to sit in the water for 20 minutes. Drain.

4. In a medium bowl, combine the ricotta, 1 cup of the Parmesan, the egg, salt, and pepper to taste. Set aside.

5. Ladle one-third of the sauce into a 9 x 13-inch baking dish. Add layers as follows: half the lasagna noodles, half the mozzarella, half the basil, half the ricotta mixture, and one half of the remaining sauce. Add the rest of the noodles, mozzarella, basil, ricotta, and finally, sauce. Top with the remaining ¼ cup of the Parmesan.

6. Bake for 30 minutes, until the sauce is bubbling and the cheese begins to brown. Let cool for 10 minutes and serve.

Chicken Mac and Cheese

Yield: Serves 2 | Prep Time: 15 minutes | Cook Time: 30 minutes

Everyone loves mac and cheese. Adding chicken adds that protein you need to make this a complete meal and elevates a ho-hum side dish. Serve with a green salad.

INGREDIENTS

2 boneless, skinless chicken breasts

Salt and freshly ground black pepper

8 ounces elbow noodles

3 tablespoons unsalted butter

3 tablespoons all-purpose flour

2¾ cups whole milk

2 cups shredded sharp cheddar cheese

Chopped chives for garnish

DIRECTIONS

1. Preheat the oven to 400°F. Line a baking sheet with parchment paper.

2. Place the chicken breasts on the baking sheet, season with salt and pepper, and bake for 20 minutes. Meanwhile, bring a large pot of water to a boil. Add the noodles and cook until al dente. Drain and set aside.

3. While the pasta cooks, melt the butter in a large saucepan over medium heat. Add the flour and whisk until smooth. Cook for 1 to 2 minutes, then add the milk and cook until the sauce thickens, about 5 minutes. Add the cheddar and whisk well.

4. Cut the chicken into cubes. Add the pasta, season with salt and pepper to taste, and stir to combine. Garnish with chopped chives and serve.

Bacon Ranch Chicken Dinner

Yield: Serves 4 | Prep Time: 15 minutes | Cook Time: 30 minutes

Pasta. Ranch. Cheese. Bacon. What's not to love? This hearty pasta bake comes together quickly and will satisfy even the pickiest of eaters. Add as much or as little hot sauce as you like, but I think the spicier this dish is, the better.

INGREDIENTS

8 ounces cavatappi

2 slices bacon, chopped

1 pound shredded rotisserie chicken

Salt and freshly ground black pepper

1 (12-ounce) can evaporated milk

1 (1-ounce) packet ranch dressing and seasoning mix

½ cup Frank's RedHot Sauce

2 cups shredded cheddar cheese

DIRECTIONS

1. Preheat the oven 350°F. Lightly coat an 8 x 8-inch baking dish with cooking spray and set aside.

2. Bring a large pot of water to a boil. Add the cavatappi and cook until al dente. Drain and set aside.

3. Meanwhile, cook the bacon in a large skillet until crisp. Transfer to paper towels to drain. Season the chicken with salt and pepper. Add to the skillet with the bacon fat and cook until golden on all sides.

4. Drain the excess fat from the pan. Add the evaporated milk, ranch mix, and hot sauce to the pan and stir. Add the cooked pasta and mix well. Add 1½ cups of the cheddar cheese and the bacon and stir until well combined.

5. Pour into the prepared baking dish and top with the remaining ½ cup cheddar cheese. Bake for 15 to 20 minutes, until the top is golden brown. Let cool for 10 minutes, then serve.

VARIATIONS

To really bring home the "buffalo wing" flavor, make a sauce with ½ cup sour cream, ½ cup mayonnaise, and ¼ cup blue cheese crumbles and drizzle over the top after baking.

Pesto Tortellini

Yield: Serves 2 | Prep Time: 10 minutes | Cook Time: 10 minutes

Some days you eat curled up on the sofa watching television. Other days you set the table properly and light candles. This meal works for both scenarios. It can be dressed up or dressed down and will be your new go-to no matter the occasion. I like to use walnuts in my pesto instead of the traditional pine nuts because they are easier to find and offer a nuttier, heartier flavor.

INGREDIENTS

2 cups fresh basil leaves

½ cup grated Parmesan cheese, plus extra for serving

½ cup olive oil

⅓ cup walnuts

4 garlic cloves

1 teaspoon salt

1 teaspoon freshly ground black pepper

1 (9-ounce) package tortellini

DIRECTIONS

1. Combine the basil, Parmesan cheese, oil, walnuts, garlic, salt, and pepper in a food processor. Blend until smooth, about 2 minutes, stopping halfway through to scrape down the sides of the workbowl.

2. Bring a large pot of water to a boil. Add the tortellini and cook until al dente. Drain and return to the pot. Add the pesto and stir to coat. Serve with extra Parmesan.

Shrimp with Angel Hair

Yield: Serves 8 to 10 | Prep Time: 10 minutes | Cook Time: 15 minutes

When you really think about it, angel hair is a pretty funny name for pasta. But I can imagine an old Italian thinking that her creation was as fine and delicate as the hair of a beautiful angel, worthy to hold the sauce that makes the dish as special as it is. Add in salty sautéed shrimp and garlic, and I would call this dish heavenly, fit for an angel to eat.

INGREDIENTS

1 pound angel hair pasta

2 tablespoons olive oil

6 garlic cloves, minced

½ teaspoon red pepper flakes

1 pound large shrimp, peeled and deveined

½ cup dry white wine

Grated zest and juice of 1 lemon, plus ½ lemon, thinly sliced

6 tablespoons unsalted butter, cut in 6 pieces

¼ cup chopped fresh parsley

Salt and freshly ground black pepper

DIRECTIONS

1. Bring a large pot of water to a boil. Add the angel hair pasta and cook until al dente. Drain, reserving ¼ cup of the pasta water, and set aside.

2. While the pasta is cooking, heat a large skillet over medium heat. Add the oil, garlic, and red pepper flakes and sauté until the garlic is fragrant, about 1 minute. Add in the shrimp and sauté for 3 minutes on each side. Remove the shrimp and set aside.

3. Add the wine and lemon juice to the skillet, increase the heat to high, and cook until slightly reduced, 2 to 3 minutes. Whisk in the butter, add a ladleful of the pasta cooking water, and return the shrimp to the skillet. Cook for 1 minute to heat through, then remove from the heat.

4. Drain the pasta and add it to the skillet along with the parsley and lemon zest; toss to combine. Season with salt and pepper to taste. Serve with lemon slices.

Chicken Broccoli Alfredo

Yield: Serves 6 | Prep Time: 15 minutes | Cook Time: 30 to 35 minutes

Are you a red sauce or white sauce sort of person? Or does it vary depending on your mood? A good cheesy Alfredo is a reliable pasta sauce whenever I'm craving a familiar comfort. The mascarpone cheese helps create a sauce that is slightly sweet and oh-so-gooey.

INGREDIENTS

8 ounces fettuccine

3 cups chopped broccoli florets

8 ounces boneless, skinless chicken breasts, cut into 1-inch pieces

Salt and freshly ground black pepper

1 tablespoon olive oil

2 tablespoons unsalted butter

3 garlic cloves, minced

3 tablespoons all-purpose flour

2½ cups whole milk

2 cups shredded Italian blend cheese

4 ounces mascarpone cheese, room temperature

DIRECTIONS

1. Preheat the oven to 375°F. Lightly coat a 9 × 13-inch baking dish with cooking spray.

2. Bring a large pot of water to a boil. Add the fettuccine and cook until almost al dente. Add the broccoli and cook for 1 to 2 minutes, until the pasta is al dente and the broccoli is crisp-tender. Drain and return to the pot.

3. While the pasta is cooking, season the chicken with salt and pepper. In a large skillet, heat the oil over medium-high heat, add the chicken, and sauté until fully cooked. Add the chicken to the pasta/broccoli mixture.

4. Melt 2 tablespoons of the butter in a medium saucepan over medium heat, add the garlic, and cook for 30 seconds, being careful not to burn it. Whisk in the flour to form a roux. Cook for 30 seconds, then whisk in the milk and cheeses and continue whisking until the sauce thickens, about 5 minutes.

5. Pour the sauce over the pasta, broccoli, and chicken and stir to combine. Pour the mixture into the baking dish.

6. Bake for 15 to 20 minutes until golden brown and bubbling. Let cool for 10 minutes and serve.

Hungarian Goulash

Yield: Serves 4 to 6 | Prep Time: 10 minutes | Cook Time: 20 minutes

Traditional Hungarian goulash is known for its Hungarian paprika. It adds a ton of flavor, and of course that fiery reddish-orange color. It's a one-pot wonder that has enough spice to pack a punch and plenty of corn and crazy corkscrew noodles to make it a unique dish.

INGREDIENTS

1 pound lean ground beef

1 onion, chopped

2 garlic cloves, finely minced

1 (14.5-ounce) can diced tomatoes

1 tablespoon Hungarian paprika, plus extra to taste

1 teaspoon salt

Freshly ground black pepper

1½ cups V8 juice

8 ounces cavatappi

1 cup frozen corn

DIRECTIONS

1. In a large skillet, cook the meat over medium-high heat until brown.

2. Add the onion to the pan and cook until the onion is translucent, about 5 minutes. Add the garlic and cook, stirring, until fragrant. Add the diced tomatoes with their juice, the V8 juice, paprika, salt, and pepper to taste, stir well, and bring to a simmer.

3. Add the cavatappi and corn, stir well to combine, cover, and reduce the heat to maintain a steady simmer.

4. Cook, stirring every 5 minutes, until the pasta is al dente and the mixture is thickened. (If the mixture becomes too dry to cook the pasta, add ½ to ¾ cup water as needed.)

5. Season with extra paprika to taste and serve.

6

Side Dishes

Side dishes enhance the meal, celebrating the centerpiece and adding flavor to the table. This collection of side dishes varies from potatoes to cornbread to carrots. Some are healthy, some indulgent—but all are delicious.

Southern Fried Cabbage

Yield: Serves 6 | Prep Time: 15 minutes | Cook Time: 30 to 35 minutes

The South got this one right, taking a relatively bland vegetable and turning it into something savory, juicy, and delicious: a perfect accompaniment to any meal.

INGREDIENTS

4 slices bacon, chopped

½ cup chopped onion

1 garlic clove, minced

1 small head green cabbage, cut into quarters and shredded

1–2 teaspoons apple cider vinegar

½–1 teaspoon red pepper flakes

Salt and freshly ground black pepper

DIRECTIONS

1. In a large skillet, cook the bacon until crisp and the fat is rendered. Remove the bacon to a paper towel–lined plate, leaving the fat in the pan.

2. Add the onion and cook until translucent, 4 to 5 minutes. Add the garlic and cook for 1 minute.

3. Add the cabbage, vinegar, and pepper flakes, stir well, and cook until the cabbage is tender, 15 to 20 minutes. Season with salt and pepper to taste, stir in the reserved bacon, and serve.

Hash Brown Casserole

Yield: Serves 12 | Prep Time: 15 minutes | Cook Time: 1 hour 15 minutes

This dish reminds me of my hometown in Minnesota: a little down home, a lot of butter, and simple, in a good way. Hot potatoes served at the end of the day will bring you the comfort you need on a cold night or after a jam-packed week. This recipe makes enough to feed a crowd, so it's great to take to family gatherings, or you can freeze half—it reheats incredibly well.

INGREDIENTS

2 (20-ounce) packages refrigerated shredded hash browns

4 cups Colby-Jack cheese, shredded

1¾ cups chopped onions

¼ cup chopped scallions

2 (10.75-ounce) cans cream of mushroom soup

1 (16-ounce) container sour cream

2 teaspoons salt

1 teaspoon freshly ground black pepper

¼ teaspoon red pepper flakes

1 cup panko bread crumbs

2 tablespoons unsalted butter, melted

Fresh thyme, for garnish (optional)

DIRECTIONS

1. Preheat the oven to 350°F. Lightly coat a 9 × 13-inch baking dish with cooking spray.

2. In a large bowl, combine the hash browns, cheese, onions, and scallions. In a medium bowl, whisk the soup, sour cream, salt, pepper, and red pepper flakes until blended. Pour over the potato mixture and stir until combined. Spoon the mixture into the prepared baking dish and bake for 1 hour 5 minutes.

3. Meanwhile, combine the panko and melted butter. Top the casserole with the panko mixture and bake for an additional 10 minutes, until golden brown. Let cool slightly, then serve, garnished with fresh thyme, if desired.

Au Gratin Potatoes

Yield: Serves 4 to 6 | Prep Time: 15 minutes | Cook Time: 1 hour 30 minutes

Any menu item with French in the name can seem complicated or unapproachable, but I promise these are as easy to make as any potato side dish you had in mind. The thinly sliced potatoes are stacked and baked until golden brown and bubbling. Plus, they pair well with so many main courses, such as Four-Ingredient OMG Chicken (page 60), Daniel's Meatloaf (page 87), or the Slow Cooker Pulled Pork (page 95).

INGREDIENTS

3 russet potatoes, peeled

½ teaspoon salt

½ teaspoon freshly ground black pepper

½ cup shredded Asiago cheese

½ cup shredded Monterey Jack cheese

8 slices bacon, cooked and crumbled

1 cup whole milk

1 large egg

Fresh parsley, for garnish

DIRECTIONS

1. Preheat the oven to 375°F and lightly coat a 9-inch oven-safe dish with cooking spray.

2. Using a mandoline or knife, slice the potatoes ¼ inch thick and layer half of them in the pie plate.

3. Season with salt and pepper, sprinkle with half of the Asiago and Monterey Jack cheeses and all of the bacon. Top with the remaining potato slices and sprinkle the remaining cheese over the top.

4. Whisk the milk and egg together in a small bowl and pour over the potatoes. Cover with foil and bake for 1½ hours. Sprinkle with parsley and serve.

Maple-Glazed Carrots

Yield: Serves 4 | Prep Time: 5 minutes | Cook Time: 10 minutes

These surprisingly simple maple-glazed carrots are sweet and savory. They pair perfectly with Roasted Chicken (page 64) or Pork Chops in Mushroom Sauce (page 96), and everyone loves them. You can play with the flavors by switching in honey for the syrup or using different herbs such as dill or even cilantro.

INGREDIENTS

Salt and freshly ground black pepper

1 pound carrots

3 tablespoons maple syrup

2 tablespoons unsalted butter

2 tablespoons lemon juice

¼ cup chopped fresh parsley

DIRECTIONS

In a medium sauté pan with a lid, bring 1½ cups water and 1 teaspoon salt to a gentle boil. Add the carrots, cover, and cook until tender, about 5 minutes. Drain and return to the pan with the maple syrup, butter, and lemon juice. Cook until a glaze coats the carrots, about 5 minutes. Season with salt and pepper to taste, and sprinkle with the parsley; serve.

Loaded Mashed Potatoes

Yield: Serves 4 | Prep Time: 20 minutes | Cook Time: 45 minutes

If you're mashing potatoes, you may as well load 'em up for extra flavor! The great thing about a potato is that it's a canvas for all of your favorite toppings. The trick to fabulous mashed potatoes is to start them in cold water. Putting potatoes in already boiling water will cause them to cook unevenly. Heating them slowly will give you that creamy texture everyone loves.

INGREDIENTS

4 russet potatoes, peeled

4 garlic cloves, smashed

2 cups shredded sharp cheddar cheese

1 cup sour cream, room temperature

½ cup half-and-half, room temperature

4 ounces cream cheese, room temperature

4 tablespoons unsalted butter, softened

3 scallions, sliced

Salt and freshly ground black pepper

¼ cup minced fresh parsley

DIRECTIONS

1. Place the potatoes in a large pot, cover with water, and bring to a boil. Cook until a knife pokes through a potato easily, approximately 45 minutes.

2. Drain and transfer to a large bowl; add the garlic and mash while hot. Add the cheddar, sour cream, half-and-half, cream cheese, butter, and scallions and stir to combine.

3. Season with salt, pepper, and fresh parsley. Serve hot.

Cornbread

Yield: Serves 8 | Prep Time: 15 minutes | Cook Time: 25 minutes

Cornbread is one of my favorite versatile sides, because it can be consumed in both sweet and savory applications. You can drizzle honey on top and eat it with sweet cream, or dunk it in Hearty Southwest Chili (page 49).

INGREDIENTS

1 cup cornmeal

¾ cup all-purpose flour

1 tablespoon sugar

1½ teaspoons baking powder

½ teaspoon baking soda

1 teaspoon salt

2 large eggs, lightly beaten

1½ cups buttermilk

6 tablespoons unsalted butter, melted

DIRECTIONS

1. Preheat the oven to 425°F. Lightly coat an 8 x 8-inch baking dish with cooking spray.

2. In a large bowl, mix together the cornmeal, flour, sugar, baking powder, baking soda, and salt.

3. In a separate bowl, mix together the eggs, buttermilk, and butter.

4. Pour the buttermilk mixture into the cornmeal mixture and fold together until there are no dry spots. Pour the batter into the prepared baking dish. Bake for 20 to 25 minutes until a toothpick inserted in the center comes out clean.

5. Remove the cornbread from the oven. Let it cool, cut into slices, and serve.

Creamed Spinach

Yield: Serves 4 | Prep Time: 20 minutes | Cook Time: 10 minutes

Spinach can be more indulgent than it gets credit for. Combining the bright vibrant greens with a little butter and cheese makes this a great side dish. You can serve it with Turkey Burgers with Guacamole (page 181) or Ranch Pork Chops (page 99), or even just eat it slathered on a hunk of warm French baguette. Leftovers can be stored in an airtight container and heated up to enjoy throughout the week.

INGREDIENTS

4 bunches flat-leaf spinach, trimmed and cleaned

2 tablespoons unsalted butter

½ onion, minced

6 garlic cloves, minced

1 teaspoon freshly ground black pepper

1 teaspoon salt

4 ounces cream cheese

½ cup half-and-half

Fresh sage, for garnish (optional)

DIRECTIONS

1. Bring a large pot of salted water to a boil. Add the spinach and cook just until wilted, about 1 minute. Drain in a colander. Squeeze the spinach to remove as much liquid as possible, then coarsely chop and set aside.

2. In a large skillet, heat the butter over medium heat. Add the onion, garlic, pepper, and 1 teaspoon salt. Cook, stirring occasionally, until the onion softens, 3 to 5 minutes.

3. Add the cream cheese and half-and-half; cook, stirring, until the cream cheese is melted and smooth. Stir in the spinach and simmer over medium heat until the mixture thickens, 8 to 10 minutes. Serve immediately, garnished with fresh sage, if desired.

Smoky Baked Beans

Yield: Serves 8 | Prep Time: 20 minutes | Cook Time: 1 hour 30 minutes

In college, when there wasn't much to eat, I could always rely on a can of baked beans. The taste was comforting, salty and sweet with a hint of smoke. I now like to make my own version of this smoky cookout dish to serve with Pot Roast (page 88).

INGREDIENTS

1 (16-ounce) can pork and beans, not drained

1 (15-ounce) can kidney beans, drained

1 (15-ounce) can Great Northern beans, drained

1½ cups barbecue sauce

½ cup chopped onions

8 slices crumbled cooked bacon

⅓ cup packed light brown sugar

¼ cup maple syrup

¼ cup water

2 tablespoons Dijon mustard

1 tablespoon Worcestershire sauce

½ teaspoon smoked paprika

DIRECTIONS

Preheat the oven to 350°F. Combine all of the ingredients in a 3-quart casserole dish or cast-iron Dutch oven. Bake uncovered for 1½ hours until hot and bubbling. Sprinkle with smoked paprika and serve.

Pierogi Casserole

Yield: Serves 6 | Prep Time: 5 minutes | Cook Time: 20 to 25 minutes

Pierogis are dough dumplings stuffed with a delicious filling such as potato or cheese, typically served with onions or sour cream. They can be quite time-intensive to make from scratch, so take a trip to the frozen section of the grocery store and make this scrumptious casserole in half the time.

INGREDIENTS

1 (16-ounce) package frozen pierogis

⅓ cup cream cheese, room temperature

½ cup chicken broth

½ cup shredded cheddar cheese

Salt and freshly ground black pepper

Thyme sprigs, for garnish

DIRECTIONS

1. Preheat the oven to 400°F. Lightly coat a 9 x 13-inch baking dish with cooking spray.

2. Place the frozen pierogis in the baking dish. Mix the cream cheese and chicken broth in a large skillet and cook over medium heat, stirring until the cheese is smooth. Pour the melted cream cheese mixture over the pierogis and sprinkle with the cheddar cheese.

3. Bake for 20 to 25 minutes until the cheese is melted and the pierogis are fully warmed.

4. Sprinkle with salt, pepper, and garnish with thyme sprigs. Serve.

7

Grilling Made Easy

What is one of the best parts of summer? The grill! But I don't just limit it to one season; grilling is one of my favorite things to do year-round. These recipes can all be made on an outdoor grill or in a stovetop grill pan, so you can grill any time of year.

Grilled Jalapeño Poppers

Yield: 16 poppers | Prep Time: 20 minutes | Cook Time: 10 to 15 minutes

Not too spicy, these poppers have just enough heat to make them a fan favorite. Stuffed with cheese and wrapped tight with bacon, they look like little mummies. I love how the bacon acts as an edible adhesive, sealing everything in when the poppers are bubbling on the hot grate.

INGREDIENTS

8 jalapeño peppers

8 ounces cream cheese, room temperature

½ cup shredded sharp cheddar cheese

1 scallion, finely minced

1 teaspoon garlic powder

1 teaspoon ground cumin

½ teaspoon salt

16 slices bacon

DIRECTIONS

1. Preheat the grill to high heat (about 550°F).

2. Cut the jalapeños in half lengthwise. Remove the seeds and membranes. In a small bowl, combine the cream cheese, cheddar, scallion, garlic powder, cumin, and salt. Evenly spoon the mixture into the jalapeño halves. Wrap each jalapeño half with a bacon slice, making sure the cheese is completely encased. Secure with toothpicks.

3. Place the jalapeños on the grill, cut side down, and cook just until the bacon begins to crisp, about 5 minutes. Gently loosen the bacon from the grill grate, if stuck, and flip the jalapeños. Reduce the heat to medium-low (or move away from direct heat if using a charcoal grill) and cook for 10 to 12 minutes, or until the bacon is cooked and the cheese is melted. Serve.

Raspberry-Balsamic Chicken Wings

Yield: Serves 4 | Prep Time: 20 minutes | Cook Time: 25 to 30 minutes

Why go to the local sports bar when you can re-create a recipe at home? I've got you covered. Toss these wings on the grill and coat with a sweet and tangy sauce—your place will be the new game-day bar. Sweet raspberry combines with sour balsamic and creates a mouth-puckering taste, which is why I serve these with beer!

INGREDIENTS

½ cup raspberry jam

¼ cup balsamic vinegar

Grated zest and juice of 1 lemon

¼ teaspoon red pepper flakes

2 pounds chicken wings

1 tablespoon chopped fresh basil

1 teaspoon salt

1 teaspoon freshly ground black pepper

1 teaspoon garlic powder

DIRECTIONS

1. Preheat the grill to medium-high heat (about 450°F).

2. In a small bowl, combine the jam, vinegar, lemon zest and juice, and red pepper flakes.

3. In a large bowl, toss the wings with the basil, salt, pepper, and garlic powder to coat.

4. Place the wings on the grill and cook for 10 to 15 minutes until golden brown. Flip the wings over, brush with half of the glaze, and cook for 10 minutes. Flip the wings again, brush with the remaining glaze, and cook for 5 minutes. Serve hot.

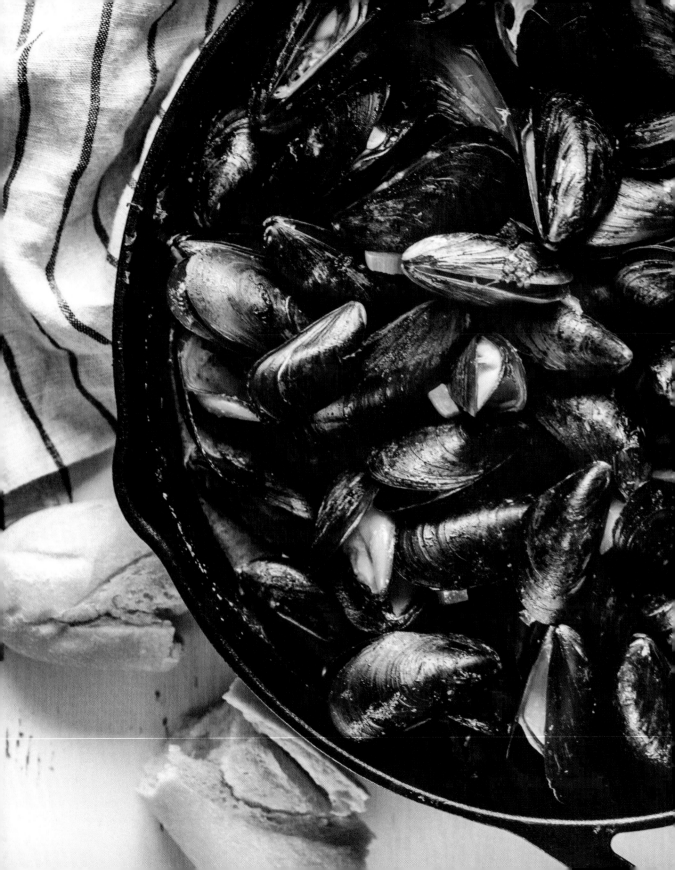

Grilled Mussels

Yield: Serves 4 | Prep Time: 5 minutes | Cook Time: 20 minutes

Mussels are a great addition to the home kitchen repertoire. They may seem intimidating, but they really are easy to cook. The most important step is to get your mussels from a reputable fishmonger. They should not smell "fishy," but rather should have a briny smell, like that of the ocean. Rinse them well and pull off any beards that may be present. When you cook them, they're ready as soon as they pop open—easy as that!

INGREDIENTS

4 tablespoons unsalted butter

1 shallot, minced

5 garlic cloves, minced

½ cup white wine

Salt and freshly ground black pepper

2 pounds mussels

1 cup heavy cream, room temperature

¼ cup minced fresh parsley

DIRECTIONS

1. Preheat the grill to medium heat (about 350°F). Place a large cast-iron skillet on the grill.

2. In the cast-iron skillet, melt the butter. Add the shallot and garlic and cook for 5 minutes. Add the white wine and season with salt and pepper. Place the mussels in the skillet and close the grill.

3. Cook for 10 minutes, or until the mussels begin to open. (Discard any mussels that don't open.) Pour in the heavy cream, sprinkle with parsley, and serve.

Grilled Tequila Chicken

Yield: Serves 4 | Prep Time: 30 minutes, plus 4 hours to marinate | Cook Time: 16 to 20 minutes

Marinating chicken breasts in tequila and lime juice overnight makes for a delicious recipe. This chicken takes on the strong and slightly spicy lime flavor, while the tequila tenderizes the meat as it breaks down the protein while it marinates. Prep the chicken one day and throw them on the grill the next!

INGREDIENTS

Marinade

1 cup sliced celery

½ cup minced fresh cilantro

½ cup tequila

¼ cup lime juice

¼ cup olive oil

2 tablespoons packed light brown sugar

4 teaspoons chili powder

4 teaspoons Dijon mustard

2 teaspoons ground cumin

½ teaspoon garlic powder

Chicken

4 boneless, skinless chicken breasts

1 red bell pepper, chopped

1 green bell pepper, chopped

1 onion, sliced

Corn tortillas, for serving

DIRECTIONS

1. For the marinade: Stir all the ingredients together in a large bowl.

2. For the chicken: Place the chicken breasts in the bowl with the marinade, cover, and refrigerate for 4 hours or up to overnight.

3. Preheat the grill to medium-high heat, about 450°F.

4. Place the chicken breasts on one side of the grill and cook for 8 to 10 minutes. Flip the chicken over and grill for an additional 8 to 10 minutes until done. Slice and set aside.

5. Place the bell peppers and onions in a grill basket, set on the other side of the grill, and cook for 10 minutes, until the skins are blistered and the peppers are tender. Scoop the chicken and vegetables into tortillas and serve.

Mediterranean Chicken Salad

Yield: Serves 2 | Prep Time: 20 minutes | Cook Time: 15 minutes

On Sundays I grill chicken, broil salmon, and prepare baggies of vegetables for meals and snacks throughout the week. While I can lose track of time taking care of errands, those three tasks always make the cut because the payoff all week long is worth it. This is my regular weekly dinner salad. It is light and refreshing but fills you up with flavor to cap off your day.

INGREDIENTS

¼ cup olive oil

¼ cup balsamic vinegar

1 tablespoon Dijon mustard

1 shallot, minced

2 boneless, skinless chicken breasts

Salt and freshly ground pepper

2 cups mixed greens

1 cup mozzarella balls

2 tomatoes, quartered

1 tablespoon thinly sliced fresh basil

Lemon slices, for serving

Green olives, for serving

DIRECTIONS

1. Preheat the grill to medium-high heat (about 450°F).

2. Combine the oil, vinegar, mustard, and shallot in a jar with a lid and shake. Set aside.

3. Season the chicken breasts with salt and pepper. Place the chicken on the grill and cook for 10 minutes. Flip the chicken over and cook for an additional 5 minutes. Remove from the grill and let rest for at least 5 minutes.

4. In a large bowl, combine the mixed greens, mozzarella, tomatoes, and basil. Pour balsamic dressing to taste over the salad, add salt and pepper to taste, and toss to combine. (You may have leftover dressing.)

5. Divide the salad evenly between 2 plates, top each salad with a chicken breast, and serve with lemon slices and green olives.

Marinated Steak Kebabs

Yield: Serves 4 | Prep Time: 4 to 6 hours marinade time | Cook Time: 15 to 20 minutes

I grew up on a cattle and corn farm in Minnesota, and I have a lot of respect for cows. I appreciate their gentle beauty, watching them wander the pastures. I love preparing steak in a simple way that enhances its flavor, versus focusing on what covers it. This recipe is straightforward, but it highlights the taste of the steak.

INGREDIENTS

1 cup beer

2 tablespoons lime juice

2 tablespoons packed light brown sugar

1 tablespoon Dijon mustard

1 tablespoon Sriracha sauce

1 teaspoon salt

1 teaspoon freshly ground black pepper

1 teaspoon paprika

1 pound flank steak, cut in 1-inch cubes

8–10 small wooden skewers, soaked in water for at least 3 hours

1 red bell pepper, cut in 1-inch pieces

1 green bell pepper, cut in 1-inch pieces

½ zucchini, sliced ½ inch thick

1 onion, cut into 1-inch pieces

DIRECTIONS

1. In a large bowl, combine the beer, lime juice, sugar, mustard, Sriracha sauce, salt, pepper, and paprika. Add the steak, cover, and refrigerate for 4 to 6 hours.

2. Preheat the grill to medium-high heat (about 450°F).

3. Thread the steak and vegetables onto the skewers in an alternating pattern until each skewer is about three-quarters full. Place the skewers on the grill and cook for 15 to 20 minutes until lightly browned, turning halfway through. Serve.

Skirt Steak Tacos

Yield: Serves 4 | Prep Time: 15 minutes | Cook Time: 15 minutes

Summertime demands quick and easy dinners—and these skirt steak tacos fit the bill perfectly. Everything is cooked on the grill for a quick dinner that everyone in the family will love! To help the veggies cook quickly, I preslice them and use a grill basket. Serve with lime wedges, guacamole, or other favorite toppings.

INGREDIENTS

1½ pounds skirt steak

4 tablespoons olive oil

2 teaspoons ground cumin

Salt and freshly ground black pepper

1 green bell pepper, sliced

1 red bell pepper, sliced

1 onion, roughly chopped

1 zucchini, chopped

1 ear sweet corn

8 (6-inch) flour tortillas

Grill baskets are readily available in most kitchenware stores and online. For best results, look for a heavy-duty, nonstick version.

DIRECTIONS

1. Unwrap the steak and let it come to room temperature. Rub with half of the oil and season with the cumin, salt, and pepper. Toss the bell peppers, onion, and zucchini in a bowl with the remaining oil, salt, and pepper. Place in a grill basket and set the corn aside.

2. Preheat the grill to high heat (about 550°F).

3. Wrap the tortillas in aluminum foil and place the packet on the top rack of the grill, if gas, or on top of the metal grate for charcoal. Place the ear of corn on the grill and cook, turning it occasionally to brown all sides, until lightly charred. Set aside. Place the grill basket on one side of the grill and cook, shaking the basket occasionally to toss the vegetables, until the vegetables are softened and slightly browned. Place the steak on the other side of the grill and cook for 3 to 4 minutes on each side for medium-rare.

4. Remove the steak and vegetables from the heat and transfer the vegetables to a bowl. Let the steak rest for 5 minutes, then slice against the grain into ¼-inch-thick slices. Carefully cut the kernels from the ear of corn and combine with the vegetables.

5. Fill each warm tortilla with 3 or 4 slices of meat and a hearty pile of vegetables. Serve.

NOTES

Sonoran Hot Dogs

Yield: Serves 4 | Prep Time: 15 minutes | Cook Time: 10 minutes

When I was a kid, I went to the Sonoran Desert once a year. These exceptional hot dogs were a favorite late summer treat and I always made sure we got them. They're topped with all your favorite Mexican-inspired ingredients, and you can customize them to your liking.

INGREDIENTS

4 all-beef hot dogs

4 slices thick-cut bacon

1 (14-ounce) can refried beans

4 hot dog buns

1 cup roughly chopped fresh cilantro

1 cup banana peppers, chopped

Ketchup

Mustard

Mayonnaise

DIRECTIONS

1. Preheat the grill to medium-high heat (about 450°F).

2. Wrap each hot dog with a slice of bacon. Secure with a toothpick if desired. Place on the grill and cook, turning often, for 8 to 10 minutes or until the bacon is crisp and cooked through.

3. Meanwhile, heat the refried beans in a skillet and warm the hot dog buns in the oven or microwave.

4. Spread a generous layer of beans in the bottom of each bun. Add a hot dog. Top with cilantro, banana peppers, ketchup, mustard, and mayonnaise. Serve immediately.

VARIATIONS

Add other toppings like guacamole and pico de gallo salsa. Or feel free to add Mango-Tomato Salsa (page 10)!

Turkey Burgers with Guacamole

Yield: Serves 4 | Prep Time: 15 minutes | Cook Time: 10 to 12 minutes

When you are in the mood for a big, juicy burger, but are trying to keep up your fresh vegetable intake, make these! They're topped with tangy yellow tomatoes and a touch of guacamole for a vibrant and good-for-you taste. For a quick weeknight shortcut, purchase a small container of premade guacamole.

INGREDIENTS

1½ pounds ground turkey

1 teaspoon salt

1 teaspoon freshly ground black pepper

1 teaspoon dried oregano

4 brioche buns

1 tablespoon unsalted butter, softened

Ketchup

1 yellow tomato, sliced

Guacamole

DIRECTIONS

1. Preheat the grill to medium-high heat (about 450°F).

2. Mix the ground turkey, salt, pepper, and oregano in a large bowl just until combined. Form the mixture into 4 patties. Place on the grill, cover, and cook for 8 to 10 minutes.

3. Meanwhile, spread the cut sides of each bun with butter. Set aside.

4. Remove the burgers from the grill, and set the buns on the grill buttered side down. Toast until lightly browned, about 2 minutes.

5. Top each bun with ketchup, a turkey burger, tomato slices, and guacamole and serve.

NOTES

If you do not have a grill, heat a grill pan over medium heat and brush with olive oil. Place the burgers on the grill pan and cook as directed.

Buffalo Chicken on Flatbread

Yield: Serves 6 | Prep Time: 15 minutes | Cook Time: 20 minutes

This is my go-to recipe when entertaining. It is so simple, but so flavorful! It can be made ahead of time, allowing me to mix and mingle with my guests. In the summer months I grill the chicken, but when the weather turns cool I can heat up a grill pan on the stove and still have a mouthwatering meal.

INGREDIENTS

6 boneless, skinless chicken breasts

½ teaspoon salt

½ teaspoon freshly ground black pepper

1 tablespoon olive oil

1 (23-ounce) bottle Frank's RedHot Sauce

8 tablespoons unsalted butter, softened

1 (1-ounce) packet ranch dressing and seasoning mix

6 flatbreads

1 cup sour cream

DIRECTIONS

1. Preheat the grill to medium-high heat (about 450°F).

2. Season the chicken with the salt and pepper and lightly brush with the oil. Place the chicken on the grill, cover, and cook for 8 to 10 minutes. Flip the chicken over and cook for an additional 8 to 10 minutes.

3. Meanwhile, heat the hot sauce, butter, and ranch seasoning in a small saucepan over medium heat, stirring to combine. Simmer while the chicken cooks.

4. Remove the chicken from the grill and shred using 2 forks. Place in a large bowl, add the butter sauce, and stir to combine. Spread sour cream on the flatbreads, top with the chicken, and serve.

NOTES

If you are grilling indoors on a grill pan, heat the pan over high heat. Grill the chicken for 10 to 12 minutes per side.

Shrimp Kebabs

Yield: Serves 2 to 4 | Prep Time: 10 minutes | Cook Time: 10 minutes

Skewered and charred until done, the simple flavor of the shrimp comes through in a unique way. The heat from the peppers combined with the shrimp reminds me of summers by the water with friends and family. These are great served with rice or even as a light appetizer during a family barbecue.

INGREDIENTS

1 pound large shrimp, deveined

6 baby bell peppers, whole and stemmed

1 red onion, sliced into cubes

Juice of 1 lemon

1 teaspoon salt

1 teaspoon freshly ground black pepper

4–6 small wooden skewers, soaked in water for at least 3 hours

DIRECTIONS

1. Preheat the grill to medium-high heat (about 450°F).

2. In a large bowl, combine the shrimp, peppers, onion, lemon juice, salt, and pepper. Thread the shrimp, peppers, and onion onto wooden skewers in an alternating pattern. Place the skewers on the grill and cook for 10 minutes, turning once. Serve.

Grilled Pizza

Yield: Serves 4 | Prep Time: 20 minutes | Cook Time: 20 minutes

Pizza is debatably my favorite food, and when grilled, it definitely is. Grilling pizza dough is easier than you think, and the charred taste on the bottom of the crust will make you think you are in a wood-burning pizza oven joint. It's like having a trattoria in your backyard or front porch.

INGREDIENTS

1 (28-ounce) can tomato sauce

1 (28-ounce) can whole tomatoes

½ cup white wine

2 tablespoons unsalted butter

1 teaspoon dried oregano, plus extra to taste

Salt and freshly ground black pepper

2 (13.5-ounce) containers refrigerated pizza dough (You can also use two 1-pound balls of pizza dough.)

Olive oil

1 (8-ounce) package mozzarella balls

2 cups shredded pizza blend cheese

3 large heirloom tomatoes, thinly sliced

Fresh oregano for garnish

DIRECTIONS

1. Preheat the grill to high heat (about 550°F). Line a baking sheet with parchment paper.

2. In a large skillet, combine the tomato sauce, canned tomatoes, wine, butter, and oregano and bring to a simmer over medium heat. Cook, crushing the tomatoes with the back of a wooden spoon or a potato masher, for about 10 minutes. Season with salt and pepper to taste. Remove from the heat.

3. Roll out both containers of pizza dough, cut each in half and form into circles, and set on the baking sheet. Brush the dough with olive oil. Using the parchment paper, flip both pieces of dough onto the grill (oiled side down). Cook for 2 minutes. Brush the tops with olive oil, and using tongs and a spatula, flip the crusts over. Top with tomato sauce, mozzarella balls, pizza cheese, and tomato slices. Close the grill and cook for 3 to 5 minutes until the cheese is melted and the crust is golden brown. Garnish with fresh oregano. Slice and serve.

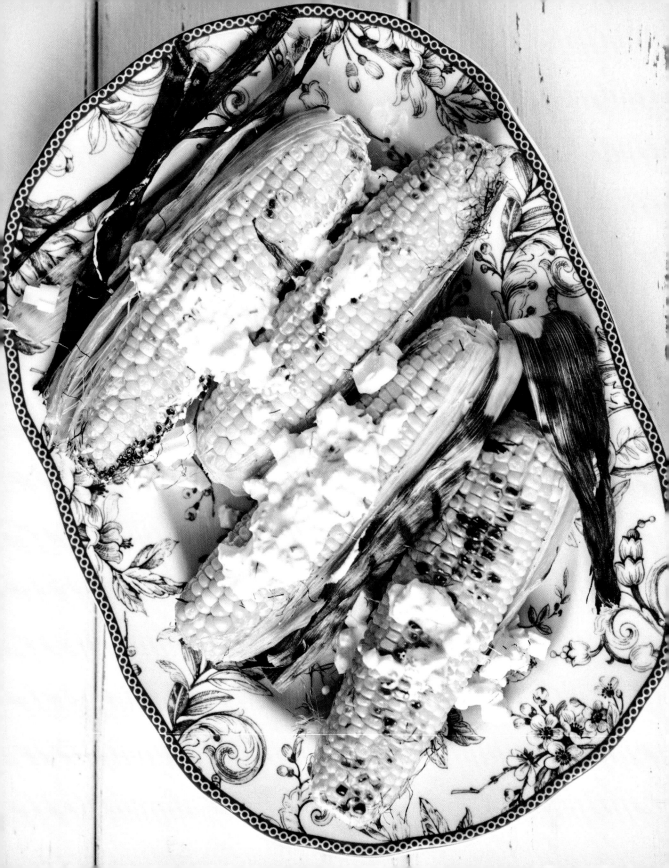

Cheesy Street Corn

Yield: Serves 4 | Prep Time: 5 minutes | Cook Time: 10 minutes

I have a lot of memories of eating corn on the cob on the street, at a backyard barbecue, at a country fair, or in open-air venue, with butter dripping down my hands as I savor the pop of each juicy kernel. Topped with a creamy feta and cilantro sauce, this is a favorite that reminds me of the carefree days of summer.

INGREDIENTS

1 cup finely crumbled feta cheese

½ cup finely chopped fresh cilantro

¼ cup mayonnaise

¼ cup sour cream

1 garlic clove, finely minced (about 1 teaspoon)

4 ears corn, silk removed

DIRECTIONS

1. Preheat the grill to medium-high heat (about 450°F).

2. Combine the cheese, cilantro, mayonnaise, sour cream, and garlic in a large bowl.

3. Place the corn on the grill and cook, rotating occasionally, until cooked through and charred in spots on all sides for about 10 minutes total. Arrange on a platter and pour the sauce on top. Serve.

Blue Cheese Corn

Yield: Serves 2 | Prep Time: 15 minutes | Cook Time: 15 minutes

Blue cheese meets corn. My grandparents, who live on a cattle and corn farm in Minnesota, might consider this an unconventional combo, but it's as good as it gets. A little tang and fat from the cheesy sauce stirred together with the kernels is a fun way to mix things up and eat corn any day of the week.

INGREDIENTS

4 ears corn, husks on

½ cup mayonnaise

½ cup blue cheese crumbles

½ teaspoon salt

½ teaspoon freshly ground black pepper

Fresh cilantro, for garnish

DIRECTIONS

1. Preheat the grill to medium-high heat (about 450°F).

2. Place the corn on the grill, close the cover, and grill for 10 to 15 minutes, turning every 5 minutes, or until the kernels are tender when pierced with a paring knife.

3. Remove the husks and cut the kernels from the cobs into a large bowl.

4. Add the mayonnaise, blue cheese, salt, and pepper and stir to combine. Serve, garnished with fresh cilantro.

Brussels Sprouts and Bacon on the Grill

Yield: Serves 6 | Prep Time: 15 minutes | Cook Time: 12 minutes

Brussels sprouts can be a tricky vegetable, not to cook, but to get people to eat. Try this fun and unique way to cook and serve them, and I bet everyone will love them. Weave the bacon in and out like a quilt and grill until cooked in the center.

INGREDIENTS

1 pound peppered bacon, slices halved lengthwise

6 small wooden skewers, soaked in water for at least 3 hours

2 pounds small Brussels sprouts, trimmed

Olive oil to coat Brussels sprouts (about ¼ cup)

1 teaspoon garlic powder

¼ teaspoon salt

Balsamic glaze

DIRECTIONS

1. Preheat the grill to low heat (about 250°F).

2. Thread 1 end of a slice of bacon onto the end of a skewer. Add a Brussels sprout and weave the bacon around the sprout and back through the skewer, creating an S-pattern. Repeat this process 2 or 3 more times per skewer, using the remaining bacon and Brussels sprouts. Brush each skewer with olive oil. Dust lightly with garlic powder and salt.

3. Place the skewers on the grill and cook until the sprouts are tender and the bacon is cooked through, about 6 minutes per side. Serve immediately with a drizzle of balsamic glaze.

NOTES

You can purchase balsamic glaze at a grocery store.

Mushroom-Stuffed Grilled Potatoes

Yield: Serves 4 | Prep Time: 20 minutes | Cook Time: 40 minutes

What a fun way to make potatoes! Grilling gives a smoky backyard flavor to the skin, and removing the insides to combine with more flavor packs a real punch when placed back in the potato boats and served piping hot!

INGREDIENTS

4 large potatoes

2 tablespoons olive oil

1 bunch scallions, thinly sliced

8 ounces white mushrooms, trimmed and sliced

1 bunch chives, thinly sliced

1 cup shredded cheddar cheese

½ cup sour cream

Salt and freshly ground black pepper

DIRECTIONS

1. Preheat the grill to medium-high heat (about 450°F).

2. Slice the potatoes in half lengthwise. Brush all over with oil and place on the grill skin side down. Close the lid and cook for 30 minutes.

3. Remove the potatoes from the grill, leaving the grill on, and let the potatoes cool slightly. Scoop out the insides, leaving the skins intact with a ¼-inch-thickness of potato flesh.

4. Place the scooped-out potato flesh in a large bowl and mash with a fork. Add the scallions (reserving some for garnish), mushrooms, chives, cheddar, sour cream, and salt and pepper to taste, and stir to combine.

5. Divide the stuffing equally among the potato shells. Place the stuffed potatoes on the grill, close the lid, and cook until the cheese has melted, about 10 minutes. Serve, garnished with scallions and chives.

8

Dessert

What is dinner without dessert? These crowd-pleasing sweets
are so easy that you can make them ahead of time and
enjoy them all week long, but beautiful enough that they
are worthy of the big weekend dinner party table.

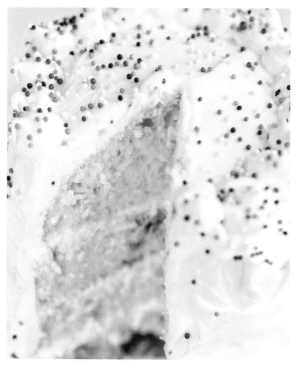

Grilled Pineapple

Yield: Serves 4 to 6 | Prep Time: 5 minutes | Cook Time: 5 minutes

In the summertime, I'd grill every single meal of the day if I could. Heating up the kitchen to cook just doesn't appeal to me when the sun is already blazing. Looking for ways to make a warm dessert without turning on the oven resulted in this delicious grilled pineapple. There are many ways to tweak the recipe and change the flavors, but this simple version is our family favorite!

INGREDIENTS

1 pineapple, unpeeled, cut crosswise into 1-inch-thick slices

½ cup extra-virgin olive oil

½ cup honey

Salt

Ice cream

DIRECTIONS

1. Preheat the grill to medium heat (about 350°F).

2. Divide the pineapple, oil, and honey between two large zip-top plastic bags. Seal and massage the bags to distribute the ingredients evenly. Place the slices of pineapple on the grill and cook for 2 to 3 minutes on each side until you can see light brown grill marks on each side. Sprinkle lightly with salt and remove the peel if you wish or provide a sharp knife and fork to slice. Serve immediately with ice cream.

NOTES

You can also remove the pineapple peel before grilling, so you don't need to worry about it later!

Peanut Butter Cup S'mores

Yield: Makes 2 s'mores | Prep Time: 5 minutes | Cook Time: 5 minutes

Not much beats a s'more cooked over a campfire. But it can be tricky dealing with a fire when small kids are around. This method allows them to help with the assembly while avoiding those pesky flames. Wrap 'em up in foil, creating little pockets, and throw them on the grill for a melty sweet treat. Instead of milk chocolate, these call for peanut butter cups, making them even more fun.

INGREDIENTS

4 graham crackers

4 regular-sized peanut butter cups

2 large marshmallows

DIRECTIONS

1. Preheat the grill to medium heat (about 350°F).

2. Cut 2 large squares of aluminum foil. Place a graham cracker on each square. Top each cracker with 2 peanut butter cups, 1 marshmallow, and a second graham cracker. Fold the foil squares around the s'mores, making each a small bundle. Place the foil bundles on the grill and cook for 4 to 5 minutes. Let cool slightly, then open the bundles and enjoy!

NOTES

If you prefer, you can warm these in a 350°F oven for approximately 5 to 8 minutes. Open the foil slightly to check if it has melted and cook longer if needed.

Addie's Confetti Cake

Yield: 1 cake; Serves 10–12 | Prep Time: 20 minutes | Cook Time: 40 minutes

This cake has become my signature, and can be your go-to for any occasion! It's beyond easy to make, and can be customized for any occasion—the great thing about a delicious vanilla base is that you can add coloring or additional flavors with ease.

INGREDIENTS

3 cups all-purpose flour, plus extra for the pans

1 cup (2 sticks) unsalted butter, softened

½ cup vegetable shortening

3 cups sugar

5 large eggs

2 teaspoons baking powder

¼ teaspoon salt

½ cup whole milk, room temperature

½ cup buttermilk, room temperature

2 teaspoons vanilla extract

1 cup sprinkles, plus extra for decorating

2 (16-ounce) containers vanilla frosting

NOTES

Frost your cake right on the platter you plan to serve it on; this way, you won't have to worry about moving the cake and ruining your frosting. An offset spatula will make frosting the cake easier.

DIRECTIONS

1. Preheat the oven to 350°F. Coat four 8-inch round cake pans with cooking spray, shortening, or butter and flour them, taking care to shake out excess flour.

2. Using an electric mixer, cream together the butter and shortening until light and fluffy. Slowly add the sugar 1 cup at a time, making sure to fully incorporate each cup before adding another. Add the eggs one at a time, making sure to fully incorporate each egg before adding another.

3. In a separate bowl, sift together the flour, baking powder, and salt. Pour the milk, buttermilk, and vanilla into a measuring cup and whisk together with a fork. Add the flour mixture to the butter mixture alternately with the milk mixture, beginning and ending with the flour mixture.

4. Mix on low speed until well combined, scraping down the sides and bottom of the bowl as necessary. Add the sprinkles and mix to incorporate.

5. Divide the batter evenly among the cake pans and place them in the oven. Bake for 25 to 30 minutes, or until a toothpick or cake tester inserted in the center comes out clean. Remove and let cool slightly in the pans for about 5 minutes, then turn out onto a wire rack and let cool completely.

6. Spread the cake gently with the frosting and decorate with extra sprinkles.

Pineapple-Coconut Cake

Yield: Serves 8 | Prep Time: 5 minutes | Cook Time: 30 minutes

Hummingbird cake is a Southern tradition, but it can be time-consuming to make, especially for a weeknight treat. This modified version is simple to toss together and bakes quickly in a 9 x 13-inch pan, rather than in rounds that need to be cooled, frosted, and stacked.

INGREDIENTS

1 (28-ounce) can crushed pineapple

1 (16-ounce) box angel food cake mix

1 cup shredded sweetened coconut

½ cup pecans, chopped

Grilled pineapple (page 199), cubed

DIRECTIONS

1. Preheat the oven to 350°F.

2. In a large bowl, mix the pineapple, cake mix, coconut, and pecans and pour into a 9 x 13-inch baking dish. (It's important that you do not grease the dish, as the angel food cake needs to "cling" the sides to grow tall.)

3. Bake for 30 minutes, until the top is golden brown and the middle springs back when touched. Let the cake cool to room temperature in the pan. Top with the grilled pineapple and serve immediately, right from the baking dish.

Berry Crumble

Yield: Serves 6 to 8 | Prep Time: 5 minutes | Cook Time: 1 hour

Last Thanksgiving, I made a berry pie that did not turn out as well as I wanted it to. We ended up eating it in bowls with ice cream, and it made me think: Why not make a dessert that is sort of a mess but on purpose? This berry crumble, served in a bowl with any flavor ice cream you choose, is a great twist on the traditional pie.

INGREDIENTS

2 (16-ounce) bags frozen mixed berries (raspberries, blueberries, and strawberries)

Grated zest and juice of 1 lemon

1 (15.25-ounce) box white cake mix

1 (12-ounce) can Fresca (or any other lemon-lime soda of your choice)

DIRECTIONS

1. Preheat the oven to 350°F.

2. Pour the frozen fruit into an ungreased 9 x 13-inch baking dish. Add the lemon juice and zest and mix lightly. Sprinkle the cake mix over the frozen fruit. (Do not mix in.) Slowly pour the soda over the cake mix, trying to wet the entire layer of cake mix.

3. Cover with aluminum foil and bake for 20 minutes. Uncover and continue to bake for 40 minutes. Let cool and serve.

Malted Milk Ball–Marshmallow Brownies

Yield: Serves 6 to 8 | Prep Time: 10 minutes | Cook Time: 20 minutes

An upgrade to the box-mix brownie has arrived: Add in crushed malted milk balls and ooey-gooey marshmallows and bake until bubbling. Delicious warm and served with ice cream, this dessert adds a little creativity to your favorite brownies.

INGREDIENTS

1 (18-ounce) box brownie mix

2 cups mini marshmallows

1 cup malted milk balls, crushed

Ice cream

DIRECTIONS

Preheat the oven and prepare an 8 X 8-inch baking pan according to the instructions on the brownie mix box. Mix the brownie batter according to the package instructions, being sure not to overmix. Add the marshmallows and malted milk balls. Bake as directed. Serve warm with ice cream.

Lemon-Honey Cheesecake

Yield: Serves 8 to 10 | Prep Time: 15 minutes | Chill Time: 5 hours

Standard cheesecakes are delicious—don't get me wrong. But this simple twist, with citrus and sweet honey, is a fun way to change up the everyday. The best part of this cheesecake is that you don't have to bake it.

INGREDIENTS

2 sleeves of graham crackers, crushed

4 tablespoons unsalted butter, melted

2 (8-ounce) packages cream cheese, room temperature

1 teaspoon vanilla extract

1 cup powdered sugar

½ cup sour cream

¾ cup heavy whipping cream, cold

Lemon slices

Grated zest of 1 lemon

½ cup honey

DIRECTIONS

1. Spray a 9-inch springform pan with cooking spray. In a medium bowl, combine the graham crackers and melted butter. Press into the bottom of the springform pan.

2. In the bowl of a stand mixer, beat the cream cheese, vanilla, and powdered sugar until smooth. Add the sour cream and whipping cream. Beat until thick and creamy, about 5 minutes. Pour the filling over the crust and refrigerate for at least 5 hours, or overnight.

3. When ready to serve, top with lemon zest and lemon slices and drizzle with honey.

Angel Food Cake

Yield: 1 cake; Serves 10–12 | Prep Time: 15 minutes | Cook Time: 45 minutes

Angel food cake is light as air, sweet without being overly sweet, and because it's mostly just egg whites, you can have a huge piece and not feel guilty about it. The texture is truly unique, thanks to those egg whites, and you can serve it with anything—berries, citrus, whipped topping, or ice cream. The possibilities for angel food cake are endless.

INGREDIENTS

1 cup all-purpose flour

1½ cups sugar

12 large egg whites, room temperature

½ teaspoon salt

1 teaspoon vanilla extract

1½ teaspoons cream of tartar

1 (12-ounce) container whipped topping

DIRECTIONS

1. Preheat the oven to 325°F.

2. Whisk the flour and ¾ cup of the sugar together and set aside.

3. In the clean, dry bowl of a stand mixer, combine the egg whites, salt, and vanilla. Whip until the mixture is just frothy, then sprinkle the cream of tartar on top and whip until the mixture forms stiff, glossy peaks. Add the remaining ¾ cup sugar, ¼ cup at a time. Remove the bowl from the mixer and gradually fold in the flour mixture.

4. Spoon the batter into a 10-inch angel food cake pan and bake for 45 minutes.

5. Remove the cake from the oven, and set it upside down with a bottle through its center cone to keep its top from flattening on the counter. Let the cake cool for 2 hours, then remove from the pan and serve with plenty of whipped topping.

Cherry Pie

Yield: 1 pie; Serves 8–10 | Prep Time: 5 minutes | Cook Time: 40 minutes

Nothing says summer, Fourth of July, picnics, and backyard barbecues like a cherry pie. Whether topped with a lattice crust or stars and other shapes, this pie adds a neat twist on the original with a hint of orange and almond to spruce up the flavor.

INGREDIENTS

1 (2-crust) package store-bought pie crust, thawed if frozen

1 (21-ounce) can cherry pie filling

Grated zest of 1 orange

¼ teaspoon almond extract

Pinch salt

1 tablespoon unsalted butter, cut in pieces

1 large egg

1 tablespoon whole milk

Raw sugar, for sprinkling (optional)

DIRECTIONS

1. Preheat the oven to 400°F.

2. Roll 1 crust out and fit into a 9-inch pie pan. In a large bowl, mix the pie filling with orange zest, almond extract, and salt. Pour the mixture into the prepared crust. Dot the top of the filling with pieces of butter.

3. Roll out the second pie crust and cut strips of the pie crust to create a lattice top or use cookie cutters to make shapes. Arrange the lattice or shapes on the pie and crimp the edges if necessary. Whisk the egg and milk together and lightly brush on the pie. Sprinkle raw sugar, if using, over the top.

4. Place the pie on a cookie sheet to catch any potential overflow. Bake for 35 to 40 minutes, until the filling is bubbling and the crust is browned. (Check the pie halfway through baking and cover loosely with foil if the crust is browning too much.) Let cool to room temperature, about 3 hours, and then serve.

Dark Chocolate Bacon Espresso Bark

Yield: Serves 6 to 8 | Prep Time: 5 minutes | Cook Time: 5 minutes

Four ingredients—dark chocolate, bacon, espresso beans, and sea salt—come together into one bite and this harmony is hard to describe beyond one simple word: decadent. Salty bacon combines with bitter beans and bold sweet chocolate to give you every flavor you need in one treat. This will keep for weeks, making it an ideal food gift. Try making some for Dad this Father's Day—trust me, he'll love it!

INGREDIENTS

4 cups dark chocolate chips

3 slices bacon, cooked and crumbled

2 tablespoons whole espresso beans

1 tablespoon flaked sea salt

DIRECTIONS

1. Line a baking sheet with parchment paper. Set aside.

2. Place the chocolate in a large microwave-safe bowl and microwave until melted and smooth, stirring every 30 seconds.

3. Pour the chocolate onto the prepared baking sheet and spread into an even layer.

4. Sprinkle the bacon, espresso beans, and sea salt evenly over the surface.

5. Let the chocolate harden. (To speed the process, you may place the baking sheet in the fridge or freezer, but this does affect the glossiness of the finished product.)

6. Once hard, break into individual serving pieces.

Lemon Bars

Yield: Serves 6 to 8 | Prep Time: 15 minutes | Cook Time: 6 minutes | Chill Time: 2 hours

These taste like a fresh glass of lemonade, in bar form. Easy to make, with a graham cracker crust, they're a perfect dessert for everyone. Store in the fridge and the cold lemon burst will remind you of that ice-cold beverage you buy from a sidewalk stand in the summer.

INGREDIENTS

1¼ cups granulated sugar

4 large eggs

Grated zest of 1 lemon plus 1 cup lemon juice

8 tablespoons unsalted butter, melted

1 (9-inch) graham cracker crust

Powdered sugar

DIRECTIONS

1. In a medium microwave-safe bowl, whisk together the granulated sugar and eggs. Pour in the lemon juice and melted butter and stir to combine.

2. Microwave, checking every minute and stirring with a spoon, until the lemon curd coats the back of the spoon, about 6 minutes. Pour into the crust and refrigerate for 2 hours.

3. Remove from the freezer and sprinkle with the lemon zest and as much powdered sugar as you desire. Slice into squares and serve on a pretty platter.

Caramel Crunch Cracker Bars

Yield: 24 bars | Prep Time: 20 minutes | Cook Time: 10 minutes | Chill Time: 1 hour

What I love about this interactive dessert is that you make it whole, on a baking sheet, and when it's time to eat (after dinner of course), you can encourage guests of all ages to break it apart, with a hammer or their fingers.

INGREDIENTS

80 saltines or club crackers

1 cup (2 sticks) unsalted butter

1 cup packed light brown sugar

½ cup whole milk

⅓ cup granulated sugar

1 teaspoon vanilla extract

1 cup semisweet chocolate chips

1 cup bittersweet chocolate chips

1 cup almonds, toasted and chopped

Sea salt

DIRECTIONS

1. Line a baking sheet with aluminum foil, leaving an overhang.

2. Line the baking sheet with 1 layer of crackers, cutting to fit if needed.

3. In a medium saucepan, melt the butter over medium heat. Add the brown sugar, milk, granulated sugar, and vanilla and bring to a boil. Cook for 5 minutes, stirring constantly. Pour half of the mixture over the crackers and arrange another layer of crackers on top.

4. Pour the remaining mixture over the crackers and top with a third layer of crackers.

5. Combine the chocolate chips in a microwave-safe bowl or saucepan and melt gently. Pour the melted chocolate over the crackers and spread evenly. Scatter the almonds over the chocolate and add a sprinkle of sea salt.

6. Chill for at least 1 hour before lifting the dessert from the baking sheet and breaking into bars.

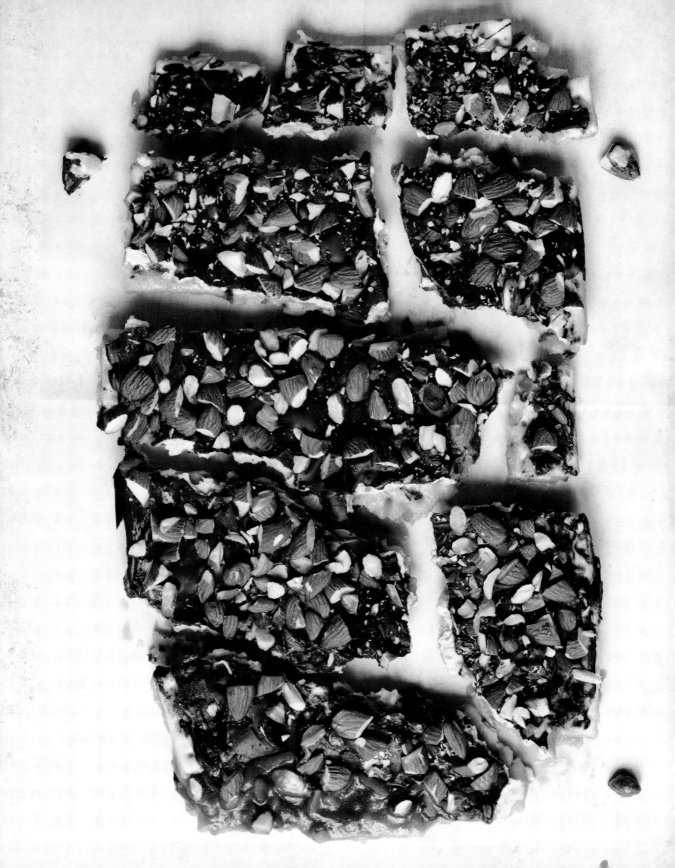

Super Chewy Chocolate Brownies

Yield: Serves 8 | Prep Time: 15 minutes | Cook Time: 30 minutes

Chocolate cures all woes! At least, that is my gospel. These brownies are packed full of chocolate and, to really gild the lily, topped with fudgy frosting.

INGREDIENTS

1¼ cups sugar

5 tablespoons unsalted butter

¾ cup unsweetened cocoa powder

⅓ cup vegetable oil

2 large eggs

1 teaspoon vanilla extract

½ cup all-purpose flour

⅛ teaspoon baking soda

¼ teaspoon salt

1 cup semisweet chocolate chips

1 (16-ounce) container whipped chocolate frosting

DIRECTIONS

1. Preheat the oven to 325°F. Line an 8 x 8-inch pan with parchment paper or coat with cooking spray.

2. Place the sugar and butter in a large microwave-safe bowl. Microwave until the butter is melted, about 1 minute. Stir in the cocoa and oil. Let cool for about 5 minutes, then whisk in the eggs and vanilla. Stir in the flour, baking soda, and salt until combined, then stir in the chocolate chips.

3. Spread the brownie batter into the prepared pan. Bake for 30 minutes, or until the top looks set and a knife inserted into the center has moist crumbs attached. Do not overcook. Let cool completely. Spread the frosting over the top. Serve.

Acknowledgments

I met a man who adores that I adore balloons. Our house is covered in confetti, I make cakes for no reason, and I rearrange flowers fifteen times, just because. I met a man who supports, without understanding and without a doubt, what I do and what I love. His favorite time of day is dinnertime, particularly on the weekends, when a fresh drink is poured and the country music comes on. I met him when I was a kid; we grew up together and many years later we began our own family. We have dined, cooked, created, and made messes together, and every dinner has taught me more than the one before. He has taught me love and brought me love, and he makes dinner a perfect end to a day, and an even better start to an evening.

His mother, whom we call Supermom (and that she is), has done something pretty similar for me. Whenever I'm in need of everyday dinner ideas, I call Deb. She's not formally trained, but believe me when I say she is a far better cook than I am.

Her love for recipe experimentation, her passion for life, and her kindness and generosity toward her friends, her family, and complete strangers are incredible to watch, as her execution in all categories is spot-on. Her smile is contagious and her attitude is admirable.

These two, as those who know them know, make a meal a meal. I forgot what dinner was, and then I met them. Thank you to my husband, Alex, and his mother, Deb.

Thank you to my incredible culinary and creative team at Prime Publishing. Megan von Schönhoff and Tom Krawczyk, my photographers. Chris Hammond, Judith Hines, and Marlene Stolfo, my culinary test kitchen geniuses. To word masters and editors Bryn Clark and Jessica Thelander. And to my amazing editor and friend, Kara Rota. This book was a team effort, filled with collaboration and creativity that reached no limits.

Index

About the Author

After receiving her master's in culinary arts at Auguste Escoffier in Avignon, France, Addie Gundry stayed in France to learn from Christian Etienne at his three-Michelin-star restaurant. Upon leaving France, she spent the next several years working with restaurant groups. She worked in the kitchen for Daniel Boulud and moved coast to coast with Thomas Keller building a career in management, restaurant openings, and brand development. She later joined Martha Stewart Living Omnimedia, where she worked with the editorial team as well as in marketing and sales. While living in New York, Addie completed her bachelor's degree in organizational behavior. Upon leaving New York, Addie joined gravitytank, an innovation consultancy in Chicago. As a culinary designer at gravitytank, Addie designed new food products for companies, large and small. She created edible prototypes for clients and research participants to taste and experience, some of which you may see in stores today. In 2015, she debuted on the Food Network, where she competed on *Cutthroat Kitchen*, and won!

Addie is the executive producer for RecipeLion. She oversees and creates culinary content for multiple Web platforms and communities, leads video strategy, and oversees the production of in-print books. Addie is passionate about taking easy recipes and making them elegant; she calls this Easy Elegant Entertaining.

Addie and her husband live in Lake Forest, Illinois, with their happy puppy, Paisley. Addie is actively involved with youth culinary programs in the Chicagoland area and serves on the board of a bakery and catering company that employs at-risk youth. She is a healthy-food teacher for first-graders in a low-income school district, and she loves encouraging kids to be creative in the kitchen.

Addie makes dinner every night. It's never perfect but usually delicious—and always fun.